Shipping Greatness

*Practical lessons on building
and launching outstanding software,
learned on the job at Google
and Amazon*

Chris Vander Mey

O'REILLY®

BEIJING · CAMBRIDGE · FARNHAM · KÖLN · SEBASTOPOL · TOKYO

SHIPPING GREATNESS
by Chris Vander Mey

Published by O'Reilly Media, Inc., 1005 Gravenstein Highway North, Sebastopol, CA 95472.

O'Reilly books may be purchased for educational, business, or sales promotional use. Online editions are also available for most titles (*safari.oreilly.com*). For more information, contact our corporate/institutional sales department: (800) 998-9938 or *corporate@oreilly .com*.

Editor: Andy Oram	**Proofreader:** Kiel Van Horn
Production Editors: Iris Febres and Holly Bauer	**Cover Designer:** Mark Paglietti
	Interior Designer: Monica Kamsvaag
Copyeditor: Rachel Monaghan	**Illustrator:** Rebecca Demarest

Printing History:

August 2012   First Edition.

Revision History:

2012-08-17   First Release.

See *http://oreilly.com/catalog/errata.csp?isbn=0636920026341* for release details.

ISBN: 978-1-449-33657-8

[LSI]

Contents

iii

Preface

Shipping Is Greatness

Designing, building, and launching the right software is referred to as *shipping* in the software industry. Shipping software is not packing boxes and it's not only hosting launch parties. Shipping is finding the right product, working through a complex and ever-changing process, and doing it quickly. Shipping is one of the few truly new crafts of our century. It's newer than management because managers have been managing people for a long time. Business execs have been waving their hands at strategy for just as long, if you count stockpiling mammoth bones as inventory control. And marketers have been trying to sell another sprocket or cog since before sprockets and cogs existed. But shipping? Shipping software didn't exist when you and I were born. Heck, it barely existed when your kids were born, and there are no classes you can take in school that will teach you how to do it.

Shipping software is new, but it's also incredibly meaningful because it solves many problems. Shipping solves money problems, because your investors are always looking for results before they give you more money. It solves customer problems because the features and fixes your customers need are tied up in your ability to ship. It solves team problems because nothing is better for morale than making progress. If fame, fortune, and the pursuit of happiness are the question, shipping great software is the answer.

If you can ship, you can make nearly any software business successful, and you can compete with businesses that have deeper pockets because you can get to market faster. But if you screw it up—by missing your date, by launching a product nobody cares about, or by building a beautiful product that nobody hears about—your team will be grumpy, customers will write to the Big Boss, and best case, you don't get promoted. Worst case, the next project on which you and your team work will involve résumé polishing. Or maybe polishing cars.

So, if you can ship, you'll be personally and professionally successful. But it's damn hard for teams to ship, which is where you come in.

This book is your shortcut to a degree in shipping. Think about it like this: McKinsey and Company, the world-famous, hyperexpensive, fancy-pants management consulting company, hires a new crop of science PhDs each year and puts them in a two-week "mini MBA" program. They then expect these PhDs to do pretty much what the MBAs do, even though the PhDs have two weeks of training to the MBAs' two years. The goal of this book is to provide you with the same simplified, no-BS approach to doing your job—or understanding your team lead's job.

This book exists because I needed it when I started trying to ship software, and I see product managers, test leads, engineering managers, and team leads of all types who are struggling, just as I did. I see them going through the same special torture that I underwent when I entered this industry—but I had the good fortune to have great teachers attendant at my hazing: Dartmouth, Amazon, Google, and my own mistaken ventures.

My first teacher was my own company—I was arrogant enough to think that since I could write software I could do everything else required to ship it. You know, define the minimum viable product, manage the project, iterate, release, market, and so on. I learned many valuable lessons, hubris among them. I then joined another startup as the chief technology officer, and spent years trying to make it big. I learned (mostly) different lessons there, but repeated the class in hubris. Abashed, I went to Dartmouth, and studied at the Thayer School of Engineering and the Tuck School of Business, earning a master's of engineering management degree.

I left Dartmouth and joined Amazon, where I was a technical product program manager and an engineering manager (a.k.a. two-pizza team leader). On projects like customer reviews, identity, and fraud-fighting infrastructure, I saw how Jeff Bezos and his lieutenants worked and learned to mimic how some of the best in the business did the job.

I eventually went to Google, and as a senior product manager I spent over five years focusing on scalability, business strategy, and the interpersonal dynamics inherent in software teams. I grew Google Pack, shipped the Google Update service used in dozens of products, and helped build the Google Apps program through mobile sync services, connectors for Microsoft Outlook, and data import tools. I launched Google's innovative multiway video products, now featured as Google Hangouts. I even worked on Maps for a while. I saw the company grow and change, but more important, I saw successes and failures and learned more lessons about the best ways to ship software.

The best leaders at Amazon and Google have a lot to teach. Remember, this business is new, so the techniques, processes, and tricks you need to ship software weren't developed until after Windows became dominant. Microsoft's old approach to shipping software came out of large-scale hard-goods engineering processes. The Internet made three-year development cycles, shrink-wrapped floppy disk distribution, and Microsoft's old way obsolete. The rapid iteration, deployment, and adoption afforded by the Internet enabled engineers to develop rapid application development frameworks, usability studies, and new process frameworks like scrum. As a result, most of us are making this stuff up as we go along, and the guidance you can glean from the relatively few executives who are part of the success of Amazon and Google is critical.

The lessons I've learned and distilled in this book cover the entire software life cycle because as you try to ship software you will face challenges in product, program, project, and engineering management. Shipping is not just project management and convincing engineers to work faster. If your job is shipping software, you must have an extremely broad skill set that ranges from deeply technical to highly creative, and along the way you must provide cogent business insight. You'll probably do everything from managing people to writing test cases to making mocks in Photoshop. If you're up for a challenge that's second to none, this is your gig.

To put this in perspective, shipping is a painful, confusing, and difficult job that's generally only rewarding if you're really good at it. The job is like playing golf on gravel fairways—if you suck at it, you'll spend all day grinding your clubs to bits and wandering around in the pounding sun trying to find your ball, which will be hopelessly unidentifiable amidst the rocks. But if you're a great golfer, you'll hit those sweet shots that put you onto the soft green and when you look around, surrounded by sweating, confused duffers, you'll know what it's about. It's glorious.

This book covers two major things that will help you be great at shipping. Part I describes a process for shipping that many of the best teams from Amazon and Google use. I work from the beginning—a customer problem—through the details of user experience design, project management, and testing to the end result of launching. Part II contains techniques, best practices, and skills that a team lead who's been asked to ship software needs. While Part I is arranged in the order in which you'll follow the process, you can read Part II in whatever order you like, and refer to it when you have a particular challenge.

The tools and tips herein are blunt and directional; it's up to you to sharpen them and make them your own, just as Wyatt Earp would remove the safety and polish the hammer cam of his Colt so he could shoot faster. If you're looking for an in-depth analysis of software strategy, this book is not for you. But if you're looking for a tried-and-true template that will carry you through a three-day strategy offsite and align your team for success, read on.

Acknowledgments

I owe a special thanks to Brian Marsh, one of the best engineering managers in the world, for sharing an office with me for much of the past eight years and helping me figure this stuff out. He's responsible for much of the good advice you read (and none of the bad jokes). Aaron Abrams was my best reader and the first to say, "Make it more snarky," for which I am very thankful. Thanks to Ali Pasha, Steve Saito, Matt Shobe, and Mike Smith for reading and providing great feedback on the manuscript. Most of all, thank you, Tim, for your patience, help with the tone, and endless support.

Part One

The Shipping Greatness Process

Anyone can ship software that works great and leaves us feeling great, but few of us actually do. More often than not, our products arrive late, miss the real customer need, or cause you and I to develop another ulcer. This is a problem. One of the reasons we have these problems is that we don't know how to put all the pieces of the shipping puzzle together in the right way. We sometimes forget essential steps or get wrapped up in the wrong details, and we end up charging blindly ahead, depending on luck, hustle, and good will to drive the product out the door.

This approach is not sustainable or efficient, which is why the best teams at Amazon don't work like this. It's also not fun, which is why the best teams at Google don't work like this either. Luckily for you, the path to shipping greatness is composed of only seven straightforward steps that any team lead can follow, and generally results in both success and fun.

Step 1 is defining the right product. You won't achieve greatness if you do a fantastic job shipping crap. The right product is one that serves a real customer need that many customers share. Meeting this need in a unique and meaningful way is your mission, and you'll organize all your efforts to ship around this mission. For example, your mission will inform your strategy, which is your unique approach to your market. Once you have a mission and strategy, your product will be much more clearly defined and much less likely to be crap, because it will conform to a great strategy. You're already done with step one.

Shipping step 2 is to define your product as clearly and with as much detail as you can handle. There are 10 major ways to do this, including writing a press release, building a living FAQ, writing the functional spec, and more. By the time you've completed these 10 steps, you'll have aligned your engineering team, engaged with your management or investors and gained their buy-in, and generally excited everyone. You may also be ready for a break.

1

Step 3 is designing the user experience. Working from the user out, you'll iterate with your design team to build a beautiful, intuitive, and simple user experience. You'll ask questions to keep the team focused on your mission, and you'll help glue the engineering and design teams together so you design something that can be built with software.

In step 4, you need to do some basic project management—not too much and not too little. When your engineering team has mockups and requirements that they can write code against, you will start to do some basic project management. You'll help your team track their deliverables, you'll help them say no, and you'll keep the scope in check.

Step 5 is when you start testing, because code will start coming in and the product will start getting real. Your velocity as a team will increase, and your testing organization will start to work in earnest. This is a less creative but very exciting time. As the team lead, you'll lead a bug triage process and make important decisions about what changes you can afford to take in your initial version and what must be fixed before you ship.

You're almost ready to launch in step 6, but before you release your software you need to ensure that you know what success will look like, and that means establishing metrics by which you'll measure greatness. Because you're following a good process, your team should have some engineering bandwidth available at this point to help instrument parts of your user experience that weren't already instrumented and to help build dashboards. Your bug count will hit zero and you'll be ready to measure your launch. Time to buy the champagne and put it in the fridge.

Finally, Step 7 is when you launch. Launching a great product is not as simple as just uploading some files to a server. You will need to plan your marketing and PR, and make sure that you go through a launch checklist. Invariably, something will go wrong and you'll need to cope with it; if you cope with your launch crisis gracefully, most users won't notice and you'll be on a path to greatness, which you can see in your dashboards.

Shipping doesn't seem too hard at this level of detail, and that's the idea behind the process. Each step has concrete tasks and will build on the prior stages, helping ensure that you build a happy team and a successful project.

Throughout these steps you will find that we're constantly working to reduce the scope of the project, simplify the user experience, and move more quickly from one stage to the next. Moving through this process quickly will help you iterate, and iterations are great because each iteration is informed by customer feedback about the previous one. Even though each version of the product is different, the process will be the same and you'll work through the same steps. So now let's look at them in detail, starting with defining your mission and strategy.

How to Build a Great Mission and Strategy

Shipping is about meeting customer needs well and quickly, in addition to becoming rich and famous. Your mission, therefore, is to solve a customer problem. Your strategy is your unique approach to meeting a need that a group of people—a market segment—shares. It sounds pretty simple, and it is, in theory. Driving a racecar is pretty simple in theory, too—just brake at the right point, turn in at the right point, accelerate at the right point. In practice, figuring out how to drive a racetrack at a car's peak performance is very hard, just like discovering exactly what customers need and aligning your mission and strategy with that need. To accomplish these tasks, you'll need some special skills and a very careful focus on a few important things. So let's break them down a bit and give you the tools you'll need for this special task.

Start by finding a big need that a lot of people share.

How to Find the Right Need to Meet

The "wow, this is really cool; let's make it!" road to product definition does not even come close to the wealth, fame, and success road signs. Your business likely caters to a segment of customers who have many different problems; how do you identify the critical problem you are going to solve first? Let's try driving the road backward, starting with those who are actually successful, famous, and yes, ridiculously wealthy.

Jeff Bezos, CEO of Amazon, has made a small fortune for his company and shareholders by constantly emphasizing that teams "focus on customers, not competition." The great clarity that this distinction provides is that your team remains problem focused, rather than reactive. Similarly, Larry Page, CEO of Google, frequently says, "Start with the customer and work outward." His notion is similar, albeit less focused on strategy. From Larry and Jeff, we can learn that you have to focus on a real customer problem.

Sergey Brin, Google founder and president, brings another critical bit of wisdom to this picture. He has said repeatedly: "Don't try to solve the easy problem. Solve the harder problem." As the problem definition gets bigger, you'll find that more users have a similar problem. As you increase the number of users you can help, you will increase your product revenue potential, and wealth, fame, and success will follow. If Larry and Jeff believe you need to solve a real customer problem, Sergey adds to that: you need to solve a real customer problem that many people share.

One example of how Google solved a real, harder problem is Google Pack. Google Pack was a free collection of utility software for your PC. When I worked on Google Pack in 2007 and 2008, we knew that users rarely applied software updates, because the experience of applying updates was complicated. And because the users' computers weren't updated, users had slow systems and security vulnerabilities, and were generally hassling their kids during holiday breaks.

Rather than trying to optimize each complicated user experience around updates, we built a system, subsequently used by Google Toolbar and Google Chrome, that enabled us to update all software, including third-party applications, without bothering users. This was a much harder problem to solve, especially in light of the myriad installation processes that third-party software requires. But because we built this software, we were able to reach and help hundreds of millions of users. The software was eventually open-sourced as Google Update. Based on its broad usage and utility as a platform, I think this was a highly successful product. It was successful because it solved a harder problem than the problem we first identified.

If you've uncovered a big problem that many users share, you've completed the most important step of your product definition process. More important, you're on the road to helping a lot of people in a meaningful way! These criteria—real, big, and shared—probably seem obvious, but more often than not, teams ignore them. They also form the cornerstone of your mission. Framing your mission statement around that cornerstone, so you have something that can be used to build your strategy, is your next step.

How to Construct a Great Mission Statement

Every team has to have a mission. If you haven't articulated it, the team, your organization, and your investors are probably operating under wildly different conceptions of the mission, and that will lead to failure. Your team will fail because each person will likely pull in a different direction, causing tension, chaos, and pain. I've seen this happen many times. Sometimes teams don't articulate the mission because they are afraid of engaging in the argument about what it is, but such a fear just delays the inevitable confrontation that will arise when you all realize you've been going in different directions. You can prevent this problem, and reduce conflict on the whole, by writing a great mission statement.

A great mission statement accomplishes three things—and only three things—beautifully.

Inspires

You want a mission statement that grabs people and brings them into the fold. Making your mission inspiring is important because it helps hold your stakeholders' attention for long enough that you can dig into the details.

Provides an organizing, directional principle

Your mission should direct you. If your mission statement is simply "be great!" you have a freshman mission statement, and you need to send it back to school. By adding direction to your mission statement, you make it clear what you're trying to accomplish.

Fits on a t-shirt

You probably won't print t-shirts with your mission statement on them, but if you can, then people will remember it. And if you want your team to make decisions that are aligned with your mission, they have to be able to remember it. You probably have a team full of hyperintelligent, uniquely talented gurus, but that doesn't guarantee that their expertise extends to remembering their mission. So make it easy on yourself, and your team, by having a mission statement that fits on a t-shirt.

An example of a team with a great mission statement is the personalization team at Amazon. These are the folks who built the product suggestion features that work scarily well. Their mission was to "increase customer delight." This wonderful mission statement fits the requirements exactly:

- It's inspirational. Who doesn't want to go to work trying to delight customers?
- It's organizing and directional. We need more delight. And it's organizing—it speaks to serendipity, discovery, and happiness.
- It fits on a t-shirt. Even all these years later, I remember it.

A final note on mission statements: they need not cover everything. They should be sufficiently broad that many incarnations of your product or service can fit the description.

How to Build the Right Strategy

Strategy is a topic that has been overcomplicated by consultants in an attempt to make money. Engineering leaders have also overcomplicated it because they frequently have no idea how to approach the problem, and instead start waving their hands. Most of all, this topic simply feels overcomplicated because strategy is nebulous, and it is hard to tell when you have a good one. Luckily, because we work in software, we can create a series of dramatic simplifications that will make your strategy much easier to develop.

Your strategy is a rough plan to win over your target customers given the unique assets of your company and the pressure from your competitors. That's it. It's not a detailed product description, and it's not a page of nuanced plans. It's a paragraph that states how you're going to make your product more attractive than the competition's product to a group of customers over the long term. In short, the three things you need to address are your customers, company, and competition.

For example, when I worked on Google Talk, I had a mission: "Allow anyone to communicate with anyone else, anywhere, on any device." I looked at the competitive landscape for unified communications, video conferencing, and VoIP. I looked at Google's unique assets. One unique and durable differentiator was that unlike Skype or other video conferencing providers, we could use Google's massive cloud infrastructure to provide video conferencing through a switching technology, rather than through the older and much more expensive encode-decode-mix-encode-decode process. Typically, multiway video systems like that cost tens of thousands of dollars and worked poorly because the hardware added so much latency. Google's technology was unique, and it was durable because you needed a big datacenter presence to replicate it. Nobody builds more datacenters than Google.

So from both a company and competition standpoint, it was a great fit. We could lead with our unique, low-cost offering. When I looked at our millions of Google Apps customers and industry trends, I saw an emerging market segment composed of workers who were increasingly distributed and working from home. On top of that, the conference-calling space was huge, and we had powerful assets in Google Voice that we could offer to users.

Given this data, I argued that we should try to lead the market in low-cost unified communications for businesses. This strategy would enable us to leapfrog Skype's older technology and undercut Microsoft's more expensive systems in the SMB and Midmarket segments. Ultimately, you can see that Google didn't follow this strategy, choosing instead to emphasize its social efforts and Google+ Hangouts. But you get the point.

As you think about your company, customers, and competition, pay special attention to how your product will serve your customers better than the competition's product in the long term. This is the one time in the shipping process in which it's OK to think about competition, so revel in it! You need to think hard about the long term, because if you want your product to be a commercial success you need the differences between your product and the competition's products to be durable. If they are not, your competitors will follow along quickly and offer a rebranded version of your product at a lower price point, and you won't have achieved greatness.

Now that you know who is going to love your product and why you can do it better than anyone else over the long term, write it down in fewer than three paragraphs, and aim to fit the essence of your thoughts into one paragraph. The shorter you make your strategy, the easier it will be to achieve and defend.

Here's another example. Let's say we're the Internet Movie Database (IMDb), a division of Amazon, and we've brainstormed the following mission:

Mission: Enlighten video viewers.

Is the mission inspirational? I think so. Enlightenment seems inspirational to me. Perhaps excessively so for an engineering audience, but look at how we've applied it. We can say enlightening is about providing contextual data, driving discovery, even helping you know what your friends think. So that seems to fit.

Is it organizational and directional? Yes. It speaks to who you're going to focus on—viewers. I didn't restrict "viewers" to "movie viewers" because I think YouTube applies, as do Hulu and other portals. I don't think photographs or other artworks apply, so I used "video viewers" as a way of restricting our focus. And enlightening speaks to providing intelligence and data, so the mission tells our team what kind of things we're going to do for our users.

Does the mission fit on a t-shirt? Yes, unless you translate it into German and use a big font.

Now that we have a mission that we think is good, let's build it into a strategy:

> Strategy: Users are consuming more content every day as more content is created, but it is very hard for 20- to 40-year-old professionals to find the content they want to watch. We want to enlighten these users, to help them discover better things to watch and understand what they're watching more deeply.
>
> We chose to focus initially on professionals because while teens and tweens have time to spend on Facebook and YouTube, professionals have less time but also have rich networks and strong opinions—not to mention disposable capital to spend on content.
>
> Using IMDb's unique collection of movie data and Amazon's ability to distribute digital content and proven personalization tools, we will uniquely solve the content discovery problem by integrating these technologies and building unique suggestion algorithms. Unlike competitors such as Netflix, who already have a recommendations engine, we'll integrate across all video sources and use our richer data to provide more interesting in-viewing experiences and more accurate recommendations.
>
> We will deliver these in-viewing experiences through platforms that can expose contextually relevant data (e.g., the cast of a YouTube video), such as a browser plug-in for YouTube and mobile applications for phones. We can also enlighten viewers by providing rich information about the content they are consuming, and prompt for feedback—creating a virtuous cycle in which all users benefit.

This strategy accomplishes what I need it to accomplish. It speaks to the type of product IMDb is going to offer and why the company is uniquely positioned to provide this service. It speaks to competition and how IMDb will be different, and justifies why IMDb should target a specific segment. It's brief and to the point. It's not excessively specific, but it is directional, speaking to specific goals of integrating across all video sources and exposing fun facts about movies.

Note that when I wrote about targeting professionals, I said "initially." "Initially" is a bit of a cop-out, but it's a great way of saying "tweens will go in Version 2," which allows us to have a narrower initial focus without fundamentally rejecting the point of view that tweens are important. See "How to Handle Randomization" in Chapter 12 for more on the "it will go in V2" technique.

When you've written a basic mission statement and strategy (yours may be somewhat more fully fleshed out), you should sit down and discuss both artifacts with your leads. This is the first step of getting everyone aligned and bought into the direction you're heading. If you can't agree at this level of granularity, you shouldn't move forward, because the next steps are more specific versions of your mission statement and strategy.

When you've reached a reasonable level of consensus with your team leads, you can move on to defining the product in detail.

2

How to Define a Great Product

THE NEXT STEP OF the shipping process is making your product idea understandable and specific. If you've defined a mission and a strategy, then you have an understanding of who your customer is and what that customer needs. You also know what you need to do better and differently than your competition. With this knowledge and some inventiveness, you should be able to brainstorm a rough product idea. Or, if you're like the vast majority of us, your management said, "Go build X," and now you have to use more than one letter to communicate your objective to your team. In other words, how can you make the product real enough in words that designers can make mocks, recruiters can hire engineers to build it, and you can get funding to buy donuts and servers?

As you try to make your product understandable and specific, you will uncover assumptions that you've made about customer problems. These assumptions were baked into your strategy and your mission, because both your strategy and your mission followed from customer needs. I hate to break it to you, but you might be wrong about what customers need. We all know that Amazon, Google, and others have been wrong many times. So you're *probably* right, but the best way to prove you are is to give customers a product and see what they say.

Serial software entrepreneur Eric Ries seems to agree with this approach, and makes a compelling case for building what he calls the *minimum viable product* in his book *The Lean Startup* (Crown Business). Ries defines the minimum viable product as the smallest fraction of your product that a sufficient number of customers will use in order to validate an assumption. You may only need a handful of customers to know you're on the right track, and you may only need to validate one assumption at a time. Regardless of how big your minimum viable product is, you can still follow the product definition process. You will want to repeat it quickly to test assumptions and deliver great incremental progress to your customers. If your iterations are smaller and faster, you'll spend less time guessing about what customers need and more time acting on what customers tell you—and that will lead to greatness.

There are 10 major steps to the product definition process. Each step builds on the step before. Ten steps may seem like a lot of process, but some of these steps are easy, and you can choose to do some of them (like writing a press release) only once at the beginning of a series of small iterations, rather than for each small product update. Step 1 of the product definition process begins after you have figured out your strategy. The process ends at step 10 with a fully defined and clearly articulated product that you can start to code up with your engineering team.

1. **Write a press release.** An unusual way to start, this is a less-than-one-page document that drives understanding and clarity and follows from your strategy. Amazon loves this approach. You can probably hammer this out in a couple of days.

2. **Create a living Frequently Asked Questions (FAQ) document.** This running document collects objections and details that must be addressed. You can start this document in an hour and then add to it in your "spare" time before and after the release. It's very inexpensive to build and maintain, particularly if you build it in a wiki or Google Doc.

3. **Make wireframes or flowcharts.** Wireframes and flowcharts describe your product visually and help make discussions and answers more concrete. You might spend a day or a week on these drawings. They're one of the most powerful communication tools you have, and they're worth the effort.

4. **Write a one-pager or 10-minute pitch deck.** This single-page document describes your product in enough detail for a senior executive or most venture capitalists (VCs). This deck will have the same content as the one-pager, but is used when you're presenting. A draft one-pager will take a couple of hours to build, and the same goes for the pitch deck. I find that it takes one to two weeks to refine the one-pager and pitch deck after I have a draft because I have to test them out on people and collect a lot of different opinions. Sifting through this data and figuring out how to make these documents sing takes some brain time.

5. **Add application programming interfaces (APIs) to your FAQ.** APIs are the first technical tentacles of your product, and you'll fully

integrate them into your requirements in step 6. You can probably draft a rough cut of your APIs in a few hours and refine them over time with the help of your engineering team.

6. **Write the functional specifications document.** This document is also known as a *product requirements document* (PRD, at Google), or *marketing requirements document* (MRD, at Microsoft). Regardless of its name, this is the big document. It's the bible that describes in detail how everything will work and why it works like that. You'll fill in sections by copying from your press release, FAQ, wireframes, one-pager, and APIs. To these major ingredients, you'll add spices like your capacity plan, nongoals, and clear use cases that shed light on all the corners exposed in the FAQ.

   The functional specifications document can take anywhere from a couple of days to a couple of weeks to finish, depending on your product scale and how mature it is. If your product is immature, you want to make the product as small as possible so you can test your assumptions. If your product is larger and more mature (e.g., Apple's iPhone), you will need a more robust and complete functional specifications document.

7. **Review the product with design and engineering leadership.** The goal of this step is to get buy-in from the individual contributors and solicit their advice so you expose all potential edge cases. If you can pull everyone together into an offsite meeting, you can get this review done in a day, although you won't have the more nuanced feedback you'll get from people who have had a chance to scratch their heads for a bit about what you're proposing. If you have to nag your team to read and review your document—well, you know how that goes.

8. **Test the product concept on customers.** At this stage, you need to make sure that you're solving the problem you set out to solve. You can get a good cognitive walkthrough done in a day, and you can get online feedback in a few days.

9. **Name it, price it, and forecast your revenue.** While you can sometimes delay these items and operate on faith that you'll be successful, I find I sleep better when I know that there's a solid upside for investors in the product. Also, while some MBAs will spend two weeks on a pricing or revenue model, I think you can (and should!) complete this step in less than a few hours. If you spend more time than that, you're probably trying to be too fancy.

10. **Pitch your product to the execs.** You can now take your product to your executives or VCs for final approval. You'll use your 10-minute pitch, your FAQ, and your wireframes, and leave them with the functional requirements. If you can sell your product upstairs, you can start building it downstairs. It should take you 30 minutes to pitch your 10-minute deck (more about this later).

These steps can look overwhelming, but don't worry, they're not super-hard to complete. This detailed product definition process is a very granular and linear breakdown of an otherwise messy experience. If you complete the steps one at a time and celebrate each milestone you pass, you can actually have a pretty good time. Most of these steps, except for steps 6 and 7, are fast and fun (if you're a geek like me). So let's start at step 1 and build a product.

Step 1. Write a Press Release

An unorthodox but otherwise great way to start defining your product is by writing a press release. Jeff Bezos and company pioneered the "write the press release first" approach at Amazon. The concept is that you have one page in which to make the marketing announcement. A great press release or blog post communicates critical information that succinctly describes the product. The benefit of starting with a press release instead of the FAQ or one-pager is that it is inherently brief, readable, and focused on what the real product will mean to real users.

A good press release or blog post contains six things:

- What your product is named.
- When it will ship.
- Who it's for.
- What problem it solves.
- How it solves that problem. Briefly!
- What's so great about it that the CEO will go on record espousing its virtues.

Note that a press release or blog post doesn't go into deep details. It rarely includes graphics and never includes financials. A press release is a crisp summary of what, when, and why, from the customer perspective. If you're following the earlier advice, you should already be thinking about your product from the customer perspective, and that will make the press release easy to write. In fact, all of these items follow directly from your strategy. For example, you should already know what the CEO will rave about in the press release: it's your unique approach to the market.

When I worked on Google Apps, I helped write the blog post that follows. There are a couple of prefatory paragraphs that speak to general business pain points (in 2009 it was harder to deploy Google Apps), but in general you'll see how it conforms to the requirements of a good blog post. Since it's a blog post, you'll see that instead of a quote from the CEO, I used a testimonial from a major customer. We were extremely happy with the performance of this post and how well aligned our product was with customer needs, and that is precisely what you're trying to accomplish at this stage of your development.[1]

Use Microsoft Outlook with Google Apps for email, contacts, and calendar

TUESDAY, JUNE 9, 2009

Over the last year, we've had a razor sharp focus on making it as easy as possible for businesses to deploy Google Apps. In the last few months you've seen some of the results, from offline Gmail to user directory synchronization to full BlackBerry® interoperability.

Today we're excited to remove another key barrier to enterprise adoption of Google Apps with Google Apps Sync for Microsoft Outlook. Google Apps Sync for Microsoft Outlook lets you use Microsoft Outlook seamlessly with Google Apps Premier or Education Editions.

Many business users prefer Gmail's interface and features to products they've used in the past. But sometimes there are people who just love Outlook. For them, we've developed Google Apps Sync for Microsoft Outlook. It enables Outlook users to connect to Google Apps for business email, contacts, and calendar. And they can always use Gmail's web interface to access their information when they're not on their work computer.

---

1   You can see the whole post online at *http://googleenterprise.blogspot.com/2009/06/ use-microsoft-outlook-with-google-apps.html.*

Key features include:

- Email, calendar, and contacts synchronization. For email, the plug-in uses the offline Gmail protocol, which is much faster than IMAP or other methods.
- Free/Busy lookup and Global Address List functionality, which makes it easy to schedule meetings with your colleagues, regardless of whether they use Outlook's calendar or Google Calendar.
- A simple, two-click data migration tool that allows employees to easily copy existing data from Exchange or Outlook into Google Apps.

If you read this post and said, "If I were Eric Schmidt, I'd understand why these guys invested a couple years in this engineering effort—good job!" then starting with the blog post is right for you. If you said, "This guy is a ding-dong. When can we get to the APIs?" then you might want to skip step 1. But don't skip any of the other steps, OK?

If you're going to skip the press release, then complete the next two steps. You'll end up building a one-page document that says roughly the same things that the press release does—it'll just be harder because you didn't start with a customer-facing message. Other situations where you may skip the press release can include internal systems development, feature improvements, and corporate environments where something novel like a predevelopment press release won't be met with applause.

Step 2. Create a Living Frequently Asked Questions Document

As I move forward in the product definition process, I find that I accrete tons of questions, many of which are extremely important because they inevitably point to product gaps. I immediately write down these questions in an internal FAQ document and answer them if I can. I like dumb questions because when I answer them, I feel like I've made progress without expending much effort. It's a rare and delightful feeling for me.

If I think a user may ask the same question that I receive, I write the question in an "External" section of the same document. I also continue to update the document with new questions as they arrive, so the document becomes a "living" source of truth for people with questions.

When I get a question I can't answer, it goes into the FAQ too, along with the hope that someone else will answer it. Worst case, you can use the FAQ just like a personal bug list or source of topics for discussion with your team. When the number of open issues approaches zero, you're ready to write a quality one-pager or product requirements doc.

There are two major benefits of building an FAQ document. First, the FAQ is great because it saves you a lot of email and can put out internal fires. It answers obvious questions without you having to send a long email. More important, when you get heckled about minor points, simply pointing folks to the FAQ is enough to indicate that you have done your homework and will douse most hand-waving complaints.

Second, the FAQ becomes a valuable resource for your support and tech writing team since they can organize all public content around it. And because you've organized it into Internal/External sections, they already know what they can say publicly. Building the FAQ is a great idea because it will save you time during the most time-crunched part of your product development process—right as you're getting ready to release and your team needs to finalize the support content.

Step 3. Draw Wireframes and Flowcharts

As you've been answering the questions in the FAQ, you're likely encountering questions that are best answered visually, particularly when it comes to delicate parts of the user experience (UX). It helps immensely to draw flowcharts for user workflows and system interactions. Similarly, drawing coarse wireframes that walk through the user experience can make the product more concrete and will be incredibly valuable in the 10-minute pitch that we'll discuss later. Sketches you make on the whiteboard or on plain paper and then photograph with your mobile phone are also a wonderful way of communicating your ideas.

I think the process and techniques involved in drawing wireframes or flowcharts is so important that I've dedicated a whole section to it in Chapter 4, so I won't dwell on it here.

Step 4. Write the One-Pager and/or Build a 10-Minute Pitch

At this point in the product development process, you should have a good idea of your customer, the problem you're trying to solve, and how you're going to solve it. The next step is generally to get preliminary support from your engineering team, your executive management, VCs, or other stakeholders. You want to check the temperature of your investors at this stage because step 7, the big document, is right around the corner, and you don't want to overinvest in that document if you can help it. The other benefit of building the pitch at this point is that you can state the assumptions from which you started more clearly; you're likely much more erudite at this juncture.

A one-page summary of your product and/or a 10-minute pitch deck are all you need. Feel free to include your wireframes or flowcharts and not count the space they take up in the one-pager.

At Amazon it's critical to have a one-pager because that's how the business operates—the senior vice presidents (SVPs, a.k.a. the "S-Team") all sit around a table and read your document quietly and then when they're all done, they discuss it. This is a strange dynamic to experience; it's kind of like sitting in an SAT where everyone wants to be the first to put his or her pencil down. For better or worse, it's how Amazon's SVPs have worked for years now.

Google operates differently than Amazon. At Google you need a pitch deck, even if you plan to speak without slides, because you will need to present in person and Google hasn't established the SAT system that Amazon has. You can find instructions on how to build a great 10-minute pitch in Chapter 5.

For VCs, you'll need both a one-page summary and a pitch because you'll need to send something in email (the one-pager) and present something (the pitch deck). Regardless of where you work, both of these artifacts are an extension of the press release and they contain the same basic content. The five major elements you must include in your summary are:

- What it's called
- Who it's for + **how many of these users exist**
- What problem it solves + **how valuable that solution is to a user**
- How it solves that problem + **what that solution looks like, and why your approach is durably different than the competition**
- When it will ship + **what the major milestones are**
- *For VCs only:* team profile

The one-pager and pitch deck extend the press release to explain the market opportunity (number of users), the revenue opportunity (value of the solution), and sustainable competitive advantage (durable differentiation). If you can't make a clear statement about these topics in one page, keep working on it.

It may seem challenging to fit all these points into a 10-minute presentation or a one-page document. You're right; it is challenging. Most team leads fail the first few times they try to create such a concise, powerful document or presentation. I've seen hundreds of decks from companies looking for investment or to be acquired, and very few have built a coherent pitch that can be presented quickly and clearly. Therefore, building a clear, concise pitch is an essential task for the team lead. It will get you instant respect and attention, and you'll get your message across to boot. There are detailed instructions on how to build the 10-minute pitch in the section "How to Build and Give a Great Presentation" in Chapter 10.

One final note on this particular 10-minute pitch: most of the people to whom you're going to pitch, whether they are inside your company or outside, or engineering or business focused, are going to be very smart and knowledgeable about your industry. However, they won't have any context on your specific business. The best way I've seen to present to these groups is to start with the user and move outward (see the aforementioned outline). Do this quickly and then allow the smart folks to whom you are presenting dig into areas that they care about. Your audience needs to do this level of investigation not because you don't have the data but because it's their way of interviewing you. Embrace the interview!

Step 5. Add APIs to Your FAQ

The goal of adding APIs to your product description is to explain how your team will interface with other teams. APIs can also explain how external developers might work with your systems and what kind of data you'll store. Another one of the advantages of articulating APIs in advance is that it helps you build a great platform; service-oriented architectures (see Chapter 3) hinge on these APIs, so writing them up front helps everyone a great deal.

Most important, APIs make the boundaries of your system very clear and concrete. Concrete boundaries help people understand where the responsibility for various functions or outputs lie. That level of understanding between parties enables a good conversation about your product requirements because you start from a shared understanding and vocabulary.

APIs can be very useful but can also backfire because the engineers you work with may feel that APIs are their territory. Be careful—feel out the team first. If they understand that the idea behind you writing APIs is so that high-level management can agree on which teams will own which data, and which interfaces must be maintained as part of your partnership, they'll likely acquiesce. If they don't, don't fight for it. I like to remind myself in these times that I serve at the pleasure of my engineering team, and I find a different way of getting the message across.

One example of writing APIs up front comes from a project at Amazon, when my team built the content scoring system for Amazon's customer reviews. As part of the product definition process, I needed to tell the customer reviews team how they'd get scores from our system. So I wrote this simple API into the FAQ:

```
float getContentQualityScore(string reviewId,
    string userId){}
```

This example is simplistic (and is written in some unknown programming language), but it shows a few important things:

- We'll assume that the index is not the ASIN (the Amazon product ID) but rather the Reviews' ID system.
- We'll assume that the score will be a noninteger number.
- We had the idea that we could support a Netflix-style review ratings system for people like you, so that we can give you the reviews that are most relevant. We figured it was best to put that in the API.

You may want to provide less detail than I show in this API. But if you're building anything developer facing, even if those developers are other engineers within your business, it's worth considering digging deep so that you don't expose a problem later. For example, if Reviews were assuming we'd give the content a letter grade, its sort algorithm might be completely different!

Step 6. Write the Functional Specifications Document

You've crafted a product idea that solves a real need for a real group of customers. You've pitched and received buy-in from your essential stakeholders. You've worked with your dependencies to define how you'll interface. It's now time to get into the implementation details and build your big document.

At Microsoft, this document is called a marketing requirements document (MRD) because the market research folks put together a list of requirements from the customers they interviewed. At Google, it's referred to as a product requirements document (PRD) because anyone can make them, but product managers generally write them. Amazon calls these documents functional specifications because they describe how the product is supposed to function for the user. These documents are all effectively the same; they describe in detail how users are supposed to experience the product. None of these documents includes technical details on how the systems operate behind the scenes. These details are covered in a *technical specification* or a *design document* that your engineering lead will write.

The audience for a functional specification is your engineering team, your design team, and occasionally your marketing team. Your functional spec will have nine sections, which I'll cover in detail. They are, in order of the most general information to the most specific information, as follows:

1. Introduction (Mission and Strategy)
2. Goals and Nongoals
3. Use Cases or User Scenarios
4. Mocks or Wireframes
5. APIs
6. Capacity Plan
7. Dependencies
8. FAQ and Open Issues
9. Key Milestones

INTRODUCTION

Your introduction is your one-pager. You may think it's unnecessary to include this information in a detailed functional spec, but your engineering team will appreciate it. It describes why you're doing what you're doing. It provides necessary context for people new to the project and establishes terminology that you might have forgotten you are using.

GOALS AND NONGOALS

Your goals are a more detailed description of your objectives from the introduction. It's worth calling these out, and the nongoals, so that the engineering team can organize around them. List your goals in priority order. Make them clear and brief. Prioritizing your goals will also help the engineering team make good design decisions.

If a goal is not 100% obvious, you need to take the time to explain why it is a goal. If you don't, the goal, and the ensuing specific requirements, will seem arbitrary. Engineers like arbitrary requirements just as much as they like arbitrary dates, and pay just as much attention to them.

Nongoals are useful for addressing objections or clearing the air when your constituents have assumptions. For example, if your design team is concerned that your device assumes the existence of a keyboard, you can address their concern by saying, "Mobile and nonkeyboard support are nongoals."

USE CASES OR USER SCENARIOS

Sometimes I see use cases and user scenarios broken out into two sections. *Use cases* are succinct statements about actions that users must be able to perform, while *user scenarios* are more narrative stories about how users experience the product.

For example, a use case for Hangouts on Google+ was:

User can share screen.

A more interesting use case, which would be added to the list of use cases that includes the previous example, is:

User is prompted to take over screen sharing when the user tries to share his/her screen and another user is already sharing.

You can see how these use cases can get a little challenging to read. They are nicely specific, though, and make it easy to figure out which pieces of engineering work are required. Agile development makes good use of use cases (a.k.a. "stories") by describing each core task as a use case, following a framework like:

As a participant in a hangout, I want to be able to [share my screen with others in the hangout].

This agile model emphasizes the user type and action and works reasonably well. But when the actions become complicated, user scenarios can become very powerful. For example, if we were to rewrite the Hangouts use cases as a user scenario, you can see how a developer would end up with a better sense of the intended user experience.

Jody wants to share her screen. She clicks the "share screen" button. She is prompted to select the window she wants to share, and she can also choose to share her whole desktop. Pictures and labels describe the options she has, and the pictures are updated in real time, like little videos. When Jody clicks on an option, she starts presenting her screen, unless someone else is already presenting. If someone else is presenting, Jody is prompted to take over: "Rick is currently sharing his/her screen. Do you want to take over and share your screen instead?" If Jody says No, she returns to her initial state. If Jody says Yes, Rick's video switches back to his camera and Jody's screen is shown.

Regardless of whether you write use cases, user scenarios, or both, prioritizing them is important. Prioritizing your use cases early will help your engineering team prioritize engineering tasks and optimize designs. I once heard an Amazon exec say, "Prioritization is failure!" Run, don't walk, from these people. Prioritization is a critical tool that enables your resource-constrained engineering team to trim a feature set to meet a date. Prioritization at Google and Amazon typically works the same way, and there are four levels:

P0

Can't demo without it.

P1

Can't ship without it.

P2

Nice to have.

P3

Ha ha ha!

P3 is where features go to die, and even P2 features are likely candidates for the culling. Because this priority schema applies to bug triage as well, your team will develop a common vocabulary and calibration. Calibrating importance and urgency is hard, so it's good to establish priorities and start calibrating early. See the section "How to Triage Bugs Properly" in Chapter 5 for more information on how this works in the later stages of your shipping process.

In some cases, you might want to help your team by prefacing a use case with "[V2]" or some other label that lets them know they can deal with it later. In reality, P3 implies V2, but even so, it's nice to know that nobody expects that use case to be supported in V1. It's still best to articulate the use case, even if it's in the next version, because it helps your engineering and design team envision the system they must build in the long term, and it will save you from a mind-bending mass of "yeah, but what if..." type of questions.

MOCKS OR WIREFRAMES

Because you're following a tried-and-true product definition process, you already have some rough mocks or wireframes. Paste them into your functional spec, and they'll reinforce the story articulated in your user scenarios.

APIS

If you didn't write these before, and your engineering team will accept them, write them now.

CAPACITY PLAN

A *capacity plan* is a rough estimation of how many users will use your software over time, and it's important for your engineering team. Your team will use your estimates to figure out where to add caching, what kind of servers and storage you'll need to provision, and what licensing concerns there might be, among other things.

It's very hard to estimate usage. I once heard one of the principals on Xbox Live talk about their capacity planning for launch. He said they picked the biggest number they thought they'd achieve in their first year, and then they doubled it. Even so, they were so successful that they had to add capacity in a rush.

The Xbox approach seems excessive, but it isn't completely wrong. Amazon and Google generally do capacity planning in a similar way. You start by building a spreadsheet that plans your capacity by years or quarters. Estimate both storage usage (number of posts, images, image size, etc.) and traffic usage (visitors, visitor dwell time, number of page views per user). At Google, you need to go a level deeper and estimate *egress* traffic (data leaving the datacenter) and *ingress* traffic (requests to your servers). For most applications, such as a website like Amazon, egress traffic dwarfs ingress. However, if you're building an application that uploads photos, videos, or other user-generated content, your ingress bandwidth will be much larger, so plan accordingly.

Build in buffer and communicate that buffer as an assumption. For example, you might say, "I am assuming 100% buffer for unexpected growth."

Assume your daily peak is three to four times the average usage. This number is a safe assumption because it represents the overlapping peak of US users across time zones. If your product is significantly different, like a software update system designed to run when computers start up, your peak may be even larger than three to four times the average usage, so adjust accordingly.

If you are a global business, you may want to take into account how you're going to alleviate latency issues. Will you deploy to multiple data-centers? Will you use a *content delivery network* (CDN, also known as an *edge cache*) such as Akamai?

Plan for spikes in usage. What happens at launch? Spikes generally have very different user behaviors, so you can estimate usage differently. For example, if *60 Minutes* runs a story on your product, what happens? This happened to me at one startup and we got lucky. Latency increased and we got paged, but we continued to serve traffic. It was a suboptimal situation, but we lived to code another day.

Plan a fallback strategy for the worst-case scenario. Your worst case could be a distributed denial-of-service attack or a *Wall Street Journal* article, or it could just be a datacenter failure. It doesn't matter what ca-tastrophe you imagine. You need to have some kind of draconian crisis management system in place, such as a throttling system, a "we're busy" page, or a static version of the application that you can serve out of a CDN.

The capacity planning part of the document is a great place to spawn discussions with your engineering team about systems design. You should understand what happens when you run out of capacity. Will parts of the system fail completely, or will they slow down? Do your systems scale hori-zontally (meaning that for each computer you add, you get one computer's worth of capacity) or nonlinearly?

Ultimately, you are responsible for making reasonable predictions, and your engineering lead is responsible for building a system that scales to this prediction. Like most things that are predictions, you need to be careful to spend the right amount of time on this analysis. Spend a few hours working on a draft, run it by a few people on your team, double your estimates, and move on.

DEPENDENCIES

Call out all of your dependencies, and if you have contingency plans, call them out too. The functional spec is a good place to aggregate owners for each dependency. When you circulate your functional spec, you can include your dependency owners so they know they are on the hook to support you. They may only read your introduction, but that's OK, since it's one page long and very clear!

Your dependencies don't need to be excessively detailed. I try to pro-vide a simple description of why we have the dependency and what the impact on the dependency will be, such as traffic and exceptional conditions. For example, when I worked on Google Pack, I had the following dependency:

> **Download Service** (owned by dl-eng@, contact m_@) — We need the download service to host the signed third-party binaries. We will update through biweekly pushes and signed clients will request the payloads over HTTP so we don't need high-volume SSL traffic. Instead, we'll just request a manifest over SSL and the manifest will include the signatures of the binaries. We expect that emergency binary updates will be rare but likely—we estimate 1–3 per year.

FAQ AND OPEN ISSUES

Link your FAQ into your functional spec. You could also copy it into the document, but I prefer to keep it independent so that there is always a single FAQ and you don't run into a revision problem where some readers will see the old version.

Link your open issues document into your functional spec.

KEY MILESTONES

If you have hard dates you need to meet (e.g., Apple has its World Wide Developer Conference, you might be running out of funding, etc.), add those to the doc. While it's great to call out major milestones for feature complete, trusted tester release, and other dates, you have to tread carefully since you haven't sized the engineering work yet. Focus instead on hard dates, not engineering milestones, and link to your project plan (see Chapter 5).

Step 7. Uncover Edge Cases and Get Buy-in from Your Team

The hard part is over! You've written this big document that nobody will read completely, but each section is relevant to some stakeholder, and the act of writing it has brought laser-like clarity to your product vision. Also, it's a good career artifact, so pat yourself on the back now that you're more employable. Good job.

Your next step is to tear the document apart and find all the problems. If you're not prepared for the searing critique and course changing that will likely ensue, you may end up disheartened. Don't fret. This next step, in which your engineering, design, and business teams pull at all the edges of your product, is a tempering phase. Nobody creates a perfect product on his or her first try. That's why you have a team. Deep breath now.

Your team is going to find *edge cases*, or *corner cases*, which are product behaviors and scenarios that occur rarely. Don't be irritated by these details, because like most edges and corners in the real world, they can hurt if you're not looking out for them. As in the real world, the best thing to do with edges and corners is to cover them just enough so that nobody loses a finger. But before you can even do that, you need to discover them.

Aaron Abrams, an experienced program manager from Motricity who's managed large-scale projects for clients like Motorola, says that the best way to discover edge cases is by "taking a *slow walk* through the functionality." The slow walk is a great way to approach the problem because you really need to take time to reflect creatively on ways that users will break your software or use it in a manner other than you intended. As you take this slow walk, write down all the potential edge cases and address them either in the FAQ or in the product requirements document.

In addition to making sure you've addressed the edge cases, you need to ensure that your engineering and UX team has bought into the plan. The best way to do this is by initially circulating your product requirements with your development lead, your test lead, and your UX lead. If you have customer support, legal folks, PR, or other individual-contributor-level leaders who might be interested in the product, now is a great time to have them raise a red flag.

Next, since you're doing the slow walk anyway, include your leads in the process. Treat the meeting like a design review meeting (more on this meeting in Chapter 10). The review meeting will give the leads who were too busy to actually read your document (and there will be more than one) a chance to comment. Your leads will likely provide some great perspective that you don't have and identify further edge cases for which you need to adjust.

At this stage of the project, you have one more tightrope to walk: you must acknowledge and incorporate all the edge cases that you and your team expose, and you must defend the core principles behind the product. If the product is deeply flawed, you'll find that it's really hard to get the engineering team onboard. Do you think you can sell the product to customers if you can't sell it to your engineering team? Engineers are a special bunch, all pajama-clad and dismissive of patents, but that doesn't mean they are not savvy consumers. Consider their feedback very carefully and spend as much time as you need to convince the team that this will be an amazing product.

If your team has now bought into the idea, you're in good shape. If they're not, the solution is simple: repeat step 7 again, starting with your mission, and figure out where you lost the team. Make adjustments to your product plan until it sings and the team has bought in. Everyone on your team doesn't need to agree that the plan is perfect, but they do need to agree to go in the same direction and treat this product plan as an experiment that has a reasonable chance of success. When the team gets to that point, move on to step 8.

Step 8. Test on Customers

"Test on customers" seems like a bad idea, but the reality is that both Amazon and Google effectively test production software on customers. True, some of the tests are "experiments" released on a subset of customers. And true, Amazon does staff some test teams, and Google believes adamantly in unit testing (but not in functional testing), but the reality is that lots of bugs make it to production. That said, I'm not actually advocating that you now go build your software and throw it out there to see if it sticks. Instead, bring your deck and your mocks to a group of users or potential users and see what they think about your idea.

The reason you want to perform this level of testing is because you want to avoid building a product that nobody wants, or shipping a product with one essential feature missing. As noted by Google SVP Alan Eustace, teams can easily get wrapped around the axle building a perfect solution for a customer who doesn't exist. Previewing your product with customers will validate your goals, nongoals, and prioritization.

Some people might call these tests "focus groups." Others would call them "presales," or a "roadmap presentation" for existing customers. Your UX team may think about this process as a cognitive walkthrough, wherein you walk users through sketches of the user experience to get their feedback on features and utility (more on that later). How you perform this level of user tests doesn't really matter, but doing it does. So organize three to five meetings per week for three weeks as soon as you have your deck together and pitch your product to potential customers.

If you don't have customers yet, you can ask your UX lead to do some basic user research; the lead will bring in potential customers and interview them to see if your product fits. UX researchers sometimes find volunteers through Craigslist and compensate them with $100 Amazon gift certificates. If you have a marketer who you can work with, try to leverage him or her to pull in a few groups of customers. Family and friends work well too, but be careful not to skew your test customer base too far to the geek end of the spectrum.

A classic example of why testing your product idea on users is critical is the Real Names™ project that I managed at Amazon.[2] Our goal was to mitigate the problem of people writing reviews that artificially made products look good or bad. We wanted to introduce accountability into the process of writing reviews. The idea was that reviewers would have to provide their real name and have it verified by entering a credit card. It's still running today, so feel free to go write a review on Amazon.com and check it out.

There was some debate within the company about the right way to approach the problem. For example, should we allow users to continue to post with pseudonyms or not? Ultimately, the way that I resolved this debate was by bringing the idea to a group of our top reviewers, under an NDA (nondisclosure agreement). They reacted strongly and negatively; one customer sent a flaming email directly to Jeff Bezos himself. Jeff is great about responding to customer mail, and that customer missive drove a rapid change in our approach, allowing users to have real names, pseudonyms, or a combination of both. It's clear to me that without that customer feedback, we would have had a painful product launch on our hands. That's not to say that the launch was smooth—it wasn't—but at least we avoided the even bigger crisis that would have ensued had we required everyone to have a credit-card-verified Real Name.

Step 9. Figure Out the Basic Business Stuff: Name, Price, and Revenue

Your work up until this point has been focused on the customer, the customer's problem, and what you need to do to solve the customer's problem. This is exactly the right approach. If you've followed the guidelines of solving a big problem that a lot of people share, your next tasks are a cakewalk. If, however, you picked a tiny niche problem, these are the steps in which you'll finally realize you've made a mistake.

---

2   The product is described in some detail in a 2004 *New York Times* editorial, "The Review of Reviews," *http://www.nytimes.com/2004/08/03/opinion/the-review-of-reviews.html.*

The basic business stuff you need to know at this point is the name of your product and how much money you can make from it. You need the name so that when you pitch to your execs or investors, you can all speak about the same thing. And you need to know how much money you think you can make so that they'll take you seriously. To determine how much money you could make, you'll need to figure out a price. Together, these are the only business elements you need at this point. Don't worry about sales training, marketing campaigns, or launch tricks because you'll have plenty of time to address those topics later, and they're not relevant for your current audiences.

First, you need a name that can pass trademark and copyright review by your lawyers and that customers like. The reality is that time spent working on the product name is time you'll never get back. The only thing more contentious and less objective than naming is pricing. My suggestion is to pick something descriptive and go with it.

Here's an example of how naming sometimes works at Google. Google's Hangouts is a product of the Google Talk team. That team of product and engineering leads probably spent a dozen meetings getting derailed about whether we should call the product "Google Voice" or "Google Talk" or something new, like "GVC." In the end, Google's SVP of Social, Vic Gundotra, named it Hangouts—he felt very passionately about the name. And there you have the second way of choosing a name at this stage: delegate to someone. The name of your product might seem precious, but a great name will not make or break a product, so spend the right amount of time on naming—very little.

Pricing is even worse and more painful to establish than naming because it looks scientific—there are numbers involved, after all—but it ends up largely being guesswork. So you and your teammates can spend a ton of time debugging opaque formulas in your Excel model only to find that customers won't buy your product at half the price, or that execs want to give it away and make money on ads. I'm optimistic that if your product is good, your customer base is large, and the need is real, the initial price of your product will have little impact on your long-term success.

But you do have to come up with an initial price, and you need to be able to discuss your rationale. Rather than spend time reading 300 pages of deep economic analysis that would be largely useless for most of your software products, you should understand the three basic ways that products are priced: price to cost, price to value, and price to competition.

If you write software, pricing to cost is a bad option unless you offer technical support or a software license agreement (SLA), and even then pricing to cost is generally a bad idea. A major disadvantage of pricing to cost is that very few businesses truly understand their costs. It is challenging to account for your investment, frontline support, engineering support, future legal support, marketing costs, and more. You can get accurate costs from accounting—but those were yesterday's costs, and you don't know what tomorrow's costs will be.

If you want to try to price to value, you can survey your customers. Ask customers at which price points they'd strongly consider your product, and at which price points they wouldn't buy it even if they really needed it. Using this data, you can ask a couple of MBAs or a high school student to triangulate what the optimal price is. This approach is reasonable but useless because your product doesn't exist yet. Customers don't really know if they need it, and therefore your data is invalid. Also, customers are rarely honest with answers to pricing questions, and they're not even consistently dishonest in a particular direction. Let's move on.

Pricing to competition is pretty much the only reasonable approach but it requires two things: 1) that there's a reasonable alternative to which you can compare your product, and 2) an assumption that the market is elastic. In other words, you must assume that more people will buy if the price is lower, and fewer people will buy if the price is higher (which is true of many products). Look at the alternatives in the marketplace. If your product offers a superset of functionality, charge more. If it's a simpler product that offers a subset of functionality, charge less. If there are no alternatives, see the first point: you must have two alternatives.

Like the first two pricing models, pricing to competition is useless when you have a substantially new product. So what should you do? Here are some broad guidelines that work well for modern products:

- Analyze your competition. If you can price to competition, you have a good starting point.
- Ask customers what they'd pay even though you don't believe them. This data will either reinforce your competitive pricing guesses or give you a place to start for a completely new price.
- After you have a starting place, adjust the price so that it is easy to understand. Google Apps chose two price points: $50/user/year and free (for fewer than 10 users). Compare this to Microsoft's many-tier Live365 offering, which is deeply confusing. Perhaps that's part of its strategy?

- Pick a price that is higher than you initially need. It's always easier to drop the price for customers than it is to raise it.
- Don't fight for a price. Often someone bigger and badder than you has a very strong opinion on pricing. I suggest giving in really quickly and getting on with the business of shipping. Pricing is not shipping—it's just one step on the journey. Move on!

Now that you have a price, you can model revenue. I've seen many team leads and senior sales folks end up stuck when it comes to modeling revenue. After dealing with this for a few years, I've come up with a theory of why: they are afraid to guess, and all revenue models are composed of at least 50% guesses. The remainder is mostly 25% market research culled from free Gartner Research executive summaries and 25% instinctual hand waving. It's the 25% market research, and the fact that there are numbers on the page, that turns your forecast from a wild-ass guess into a scientific wild-ass guess (SWAG). A SWAG is what you're trying to achieve at this stage of your product's development. But if your SWAG is mainly guesswork, why model revenue at all?

First, VCs and many business unit leads are going to need to have some sense of whether you're building a meaningful business. So you'll need a model that forecasts revenue by month over a three-year time period.

Second, building a revenue model exposes your assumptions and validates your opportunity. The 25% market research you blended with your basic instincts as a consumer can provide a remarkable amount of insight when you do some basic math. You may be humbled to find that your billion-dollar idea is only a million-dollar idea in the ideal case—and that's precisely what you're looking for.

Third, your SWAG is iterative guesswork. Your simple revenue model enables you to understand how the various financial dimensions of pricing, support costs, and marketing will impact your bottom line. Your model will provide a framework for you to rationalize decisions.

So keep your revenue model very simple, and don't worry that it's mainly guesswork. As you circulate the model, people will question your assumptions; as they do so, simply adjust your assumptions to meet their assumptions. At this point, your goal is to get funded and avoid wasting time building a product that has no legs at all, not to predict the future.

Here's how to build a very simple revenue model. You can find a copy of the spreadsheet at *http://www.shippinggreatness.com*.

1. Figure out the total size of your market in terms of buyers.
   a. For instance, when I worked on Google Talk, I looked at the total spend on video conferencing, audio conferencing, and long-distance IP telephony. That gave me a pretty attractive market size.
   b. Many consumer products go to market with a "freemium" model, in which most users use the free product and some users pay to use additional storage, access extra features, or get an orc-killing sword. You'll address your conversion rate later—focus on the total market. For example, if Facebook has more than 800 million users, the total market is approximately 800 million.
   c. Analyst reports are useful for this data, and if you're in a start-up you can probably make do with the numbers that are published in the free summaries or your VC can get you reports.
2. Make an assumption about growth over time. This will be your baseline. As the market grows, so will your sales.
3. Reduce the market to your addressable market:
   a. Reduce your market size to the segments you'll target—for example, small businesses, the midmarket, and enterprises.
   b. Reduce your market size to the countries you can reach. You might start reaching only the US, but there's a big world out there—expanding to other countries will likely have a huge impact.
4. Make a guess at the number of users you can reach through your marketing efforts. A simple way to do this is to figure out how much marketing budget you have and look at keyword CPM (cost per mille/impression) cost.
5. Make a guess at how many of those contacts convert to users.
6. Identify any other channels of user discovery and add those inputs to the model. For example, if you have an "invite a friend" mechanism in your product, go ahead and assume that x% of users use this mechanism to generate a successful conversion.
7. Now you want to calculate your revenue. Multiply the price by the additional number of users each period. If your product is a subscription product, then you can assume a renewal rate and count that profit.

In the following simple model (Figure 2-1), I've assumed we're selling a goat-tossing game (a classic fast-follower move). It's not subscription based, but it does have in-game sales, which is where the real money comes from. In my first cut of the model, I've assumed we should give the app away and rely on in-app purchases.

Variables				
Total Market	600,000,000			
% of total market interested in goats	20%	*addressable market*		
% of total goat market that speaks English	20%			
Marketing conversion rate ($/user)	$1			
App price	$0			
Support Cost/user	$0.25			
% of users who purchase in-app	20%			
Average In-app purchase amount, lifetime	$3			
Viral conversion (friend recommendations)	15%			
Revenue Forecast	**Q112**	**Q212**	**Q312**	**Q412**
Users				
Users from PR (new launch each Q)	150000	20000	15000	25000
Marketing Spend	$100,000	$100,000	$100,000	$100,000
Users from Gallery (organic)	30000	25000	30000	35000
Viral Growth	0	42,000	28,050	25,958
Total New Users	280,000	187,000	173,050	185,958
% of addressable market	1.17%	1.95%	2.67%	3.44%
Revenue				
App Sales	$0	$0	$0	$0
In-App Purchases	$168,000	$112,200	$103,830	$111,575
Total Revenue	$168,000	$112,200	$103,830	$111,575
Costs				
Marketing	-$100,000	-$100,000	-$100,000	-$100,000
Support	-$70,000	-$46,750	-$43,263	-$46,489
Total Costs	-$170,000	-$146,750	-$143,263	-$146,489
Profit/Loss				
Quarterly	-$2,000	-$34,550	-$39,433	-$34,915
Annual				-$110,897

Figure 2-1. A basic revenue forecast

I prefer to make the editable cells yellow (shown in grey in the printed version of this book) because doing so clearly identifies which aspects of the model are guesses. In this case, most of the model is guesses. This model shows that my goat-tossing game is not a particularly profitable enterprise, even with a situation in which I've reached 3.4% of the addressable market. Note that instead of working from a percentage of market share to users, I made a guess about users and cross-checked that with market share. I used this approach because I feel like I have better instincts and more data about specific download rates than I do about how broad groups of users adopt games.

Before we toss the goat-tossing idea, we should take a step back and look at our assumptions. The model I built is sensitive to many variables.

For example, I'm spending $1 per user that I acquire through Internet advertising, and I'm getting a total of 1.15 users from that spend (assuming viral growth). I'm collecting $3 each on average from 20% of those users, or $0.60 per user overall. So my marketing plan generates a net loss of $0.40!

The nice part of models like this is that you can easily change them. It's much easier to change this model now than it will be to deflate the budget allocated to the newly hired director of online marketing later. To get to profitability, I'll guess that I want to spend less money on more cost-effective but lower-reach advertising. In other words, I'll change our maximum ad bid so we trigger ads only when we can afford them. I'll also change to a different pricing model, $0.99 to buy, which will result in lower adoption (50% lower, I guess) and greater margin. Let's apply those changes. Figure 2-2 shows our revised model.

Variables				
Total Market	600,000,000			
% of total market interested in goats	20%	addressable market		
Marketing conversion rate ($/user)	$2			
App price	$0.99			
Support Cost/user	$0.25			
Average In-app purchase amount, lifetime	$2			
Viral conversion (friend recommendations)	15%			
Revenue Forecast	Q112	Q212	Q312	Q412
Users				
Users from PR (new launch each Q)	100000	150000	100000	200000
Marketing Spend	$100,000	$100,000	$100,000	$100,000
Users from Gallery (organic)	15000	20000	25000	30000
Viral Growth	0	24,750	33,000	26,250
Total New Users	165,000	244,750	208,000	306,250
% of addressable market	0.14%	0.34%	0.51%	0.77%
Revenue				
App Sales	$163,350	$242,303	$205,920	$303,188
In-App Purchases	$330,000	$489,500	$416,000	$612,500
Total Revenue	$493,350	$731,803	$621,920	$915,688
Costs				
Marketing	-$100,000	-$100,000	-$100,000	-$100,000
Support	-$41,250	-$61,188	-$52,000	-$76,563
Total Costs	-$141250	-$161187.5	-$152000	-$176562.5
Profit/Loss				
Quarterly	$352,100	$570,615	$469,920	$739,125
Annual				$2,131,760

Figure 2-2. A more profitable basic revenue forecast

That's more like it. We are now growing slowly. We haven't taken into account our operational costs, but on a pure product standpoint, we're profitable. We should work on driving our support numbers down, since they're roughly 20% of our revenue, which is very high for a game. More important, we need to come up with some low-cost ways of growing usage. Maybe the viral features could be improved?

It's clear that this model is highly sensitive to your assumptions. This is not a problem; it's a benefit, because it exposes your assumptions and the importance of certain variables. If you build a reasonable and simple model, it will help you understand your business and sell your product upstairs. But you also must be careful of overspending your time on the model—real users and real data will inform your decisions far more than guesswork will.

I know there are MBAs out there groaning as they look at these overly simplistic spreadsheets. I hear you, and I agree: this spreadsheet is a very blunt tool. It lacks a wealth of detail that could be added. But the practical reality is that you are a software team lead and you do not need more detail to make smart decisions about the product at this stage. You just need a SWAG. This spreadsheet is a good SWAG.

Step 10. Sell Your Completed Product Idea Upstairs

If you're in a startup, this is the one time you can probably take a break and go get a cup of coffee, because you can approve yourself. Unless you're funded, that is, in which case you're in the same boat as everyone else because the board wants to know what you're doing with their easily earned money. They're the 1%, and they feel entitled to know what you're doing with it.

If you've followed the plan and sold the product to your development team, you already know what the objections and faults with the product are and you've addressed them. To make the final sales pitch easier, I suggest you spend time *preselling* your product. Most successful leads at Google have learned how to do this because it establishes some context for your managers before they have a public reaction to your product. In environments where everyone is overly busy, like Amazon and Google, preselling is a very powerful technique.

Preselling is a pretty straightforward process of pitching your way up the food chain until you hit the folks who are going to say yes. You simply need everyone between you and the exec to whom you are pitching to say yes, and then get the folks who report directly to that exec to preview the concept favorably. If you do a lousy job pitching, the lieutenants will take you out before you ever get to the decision maker. Or worse yet, they'll misunderstand and your decision-making exec will have some potentially insane idea of what you're going to build. Be careful, because the risk of the game-of-telephone effect is seldom greater than when you're half-reading email messages while trying to pay attention to people desperate for your attention.

Another approach to preselling is to "do a drive-by" with the decision maker you're trying to influence. In such a scenario, you're not trying to get a decision, you're just letting the person know that one is coming. You can do a drive-by in about a minute if you see the decision maker in the hall or getting coffee. The drive-by at least sets the tone for the conversation you'll eventually have and will alert you to any violent allergic reactions that the individual may have.

Once you get to the point where you can pitch the execs directly, you're in for a whole new kind of torture. Take Jeff Bezos, for example. When I was at Amazon, Jeff was a well-established details guy who was also very smart. If you wanted to build something substantially new, Jeff had to approve it. I only pitched a couple times to Jeff and I'm sure I was quickly forgotten, but I do know that I never got past my first couple of slides. Jeff jumped right ahead, trying to get to the meat of the conversation. Another executive I worked with at Google used to do the same thing, but over time he learned to turn his leap-ahead to a leap-backward and ask for context instead. I had no such luck with Jeff at the time.

This kind of leapfrogging around your pitch will happen to you at Google, at Amazon, in VC, and basically anywhere you get superintelligent billionaires hearing presentations all day long. VCs tend to have slightly better manners, though, and Eric Schmidt will just do email during every second slide so you don't notice that he's skipped ahead.

So first, before you pitch to the one-percenters, make sure you know everything on the periphery of your product. This is a lost cause, but it's still a good idea. There will always be something you forgot or didn't know about because it happened yesterday when you were massaging your slideware. Accept your failure now—it'll be OK and it's no reflection on your own superintelligent status. When you don't know the answer, you are much better off saying, "I don't know; I'll find out and come back," than pretending you know. Remember, these are hyperintelligent billionaires—they can smell a lie like a fart in a car. Trying to talk your way out of such a failure will just prove to them that you are a ding-dong who doesn't understand how smart they are.

Second, go where they want to go. The billionaires are asking to be guided in a weird way, so do what they want and guide them. If they're leaping ahead and they haven't made a wildly incorrect assumption about your product, just leap ahead with them. Don't be the jerk with the deck who insists on walking through the slide that has the background of every team member on it when all the investor wants is to know how much you can charge. Just go to the prices. If you absolutely must cover something, then you can try saying, "We cover that in just a moment in the deck, but I'd like to touch on a couple of important things first..." But really, just move forward. Your judgment on importance matters less than what these folks think is important.

Finally, read the section "How to Build and Give a Great Presentation" in Chapter 10 and embrace the deck-in-one-slide approach. The billionaires like this because it leaves out lots of details but gets to the heart of the matter and lets them interact with you.

Your Product Is Ready to Build—Go Build It!

At this point in your product life cycle, you've found a critical user need that many people share, and you've proposed a unique way to solve it. You can talk about the product in one page, a 10-minute presentation, or in rigorous detail through your functional spec—even to the point where you can answer all the frequently asked questions and expound on APIs and dependencies. You've also managed to set nearly outlandish revenue targets that are inspiring and remind you why you got into this business.

Before you start congratulating yourself, take a step back for some perspective. If this were a date, you've effectively buttoned your shirt, combed your hair, and planned your first coy response when you find a suitable match at the bar. That's it. Now you actually have to go meet someone and close the deal. Execution is the hard part, isn't it?

I'm serious about this point. Any reasonably smart team lead can invent a "strategy" or a reasonable product idea and declare success, because we measure success at this stage by the words you put on the page and the promises you made in meetings. It doesn't matter how good you look if you keep coming home alone. What's really hard is driving your team to build the right software in spite of real-world dilemmas. Did I mention that you have to do it in the right timeframe? And that you have to launch with a team that loves you *and* the product?

3

How to Build a Great User Experience

THE USER EXPERIENCE IS not just what your product looks like, it's how it works, too. Shipping greatness means shipping a great user experience. If nobody can use your product, or people hate the way it looks, or if they can't figure out how to log in, greatness is out of your reach. So even though you've hired or borrowed a talented user experience designer, you can't pass the buck down the line and expect to keep shipping. You need to plan on sharing ownership of the user experience of your product. It's not your job to solve all user experience problems; it *is* your job to ensure that your product provides the best user experience possible, and that means getting the best out of your design team.

To get the most out of your design team, seek first to understand design, then to be understood by your design team. You can start understanding design by understanding the varying roles of designers. After you know what each role does, the second thing you need to understand is how to evaluate designs so that you can have a meaningful interaction with your designer. After you know what to say, the third thing to understand is how to communicate with each design role effectively, which includes understanding how to review designs and provide feedback to the designers. The fourth and final element of understanding design is learning how to communicate with pictures, through simple wireframes and mockups that you can create in Photoshop or a paint program.

Understand Design Roles: UX, UI, IA, VisD, UXR . . . and Personas

Designers have different titles depending on their area of focus, and even when they don't have different titles, you'll find that designers tend to specialize in specific areas. Even though designers are flexible, it can be beneficial to understand where a given designer will thrive, and adjust expectations accordingly.

User experience (UX) focuses on how users work through tasks and optimizing the presentation of information to those users. Frequently UX designers will build flowcharts that explain the user experience in addition to "mocks." "Mocks" is shorthand for *mockups*, or pictures of what parts of the user interface will look like. Sometimes UX designers will build *clickable prototypes*, which are a collection of mocks that have embedded click targets intended to simulate the usage of a product in a narrow scenario. Clickable prototypes can help you get a better feel for your product.

UX designers care a lot about *information architecture* (IA). Unlike engineering architecture, IA means designers are focused on what the user interface presents to users, regardless of what the underlying data structure is. For example, all data in a purchase confirmation form may be keyed off an order number or the customer's email address. Therefore, the order number is critical to the system. A designer will probably want to focus on the primary task the user must complete: approve the purchase. IA asks the question "what's the most important data on this page?" In our example, it's probably the items, followed by their quantity and price—not the order number. IA focuses on understanding how users must perceive information, not how systems must handle it.

There's generally no absolutely correct answer to IA questions, which is why team leads get closely involved in the design process. As the product lead, you might know that your baseball website's users care more about news than they do about team standings, so you would work with designers to define an IA that prioritizes news over standings.

User interface (UI) is the old name for user experience and focuses more on design of individual pages or screens. It's a subset of UX.

Visual design (VisD) is the discipline of laying out content in an aesthetically compelling and clear way. Visual designers tend to have a strong background in graphic design, typography, and the fine arts. They use tools like color palettes to enhance or reduce the prominence of information in the UI based on the prescribed IA. A good visual designer will help align buttons, text blocks, and other controls into a "grid" that will add consistency to your product. By drawing imaginary lines through the interface, the designer creates an organized framework with clear whitespace and content areas that make it easier for your users to know where to look and make the UI consistent from one view to the next.

User experience research (UXR) is a specialized subset of design focused on learning what users think about your product. User experience researchers are great at running studies that bring statistically significant and conceptually relevant data about failures and successes in your product to your engineering team. UXRs know how to select participants, construct studies that are organized and unbiased, and coach users through a study without biasing their feedback. Even better, a great UXR will create a report that provides meaningful guidance about what works and doesn't work in your UX. Unfortunately, the job of a UXR is not to provide solutions to your problems. That's for you and your UX designer to figure out, but if your researcher has ideas, you'd better listen!

"But wait," you're thinking, "how can I have statistically significant data from a group of 5–10 UXR participants?" The answer is that you can establish significance by comparing all the questions that were asked. For example, if all five participants have the same experience in 15 tasks, but diverge on one task, you don't have just one set of five divergent data points: you have 5×16 data points, and you can establish significance. If you feel a little dubious about this logic, it's OK—you and your UXR's assessment of individual participants in studies is critical, since participant selection can introduce a high degree of bias into studies. In our Seattle-based studies, for example, everyone is jittery and sad, on account of the coffee and rain. We correct for that.

Personas are a tool popularized by Jacob Nielsen and are intended to give you, your design team, and your engineering team a framework you can use to evaluate your designs. Your design and business teams will create a small group of imaginary people who represent your target customers. These personas will have names, salaries, and objectives. You can assign them any attributes that you might know about the customer that each represents. You will then use your personas to evaluate the effectiveness of a design. For example, in a vacation planning application you might find yourself saying, "Paul Planner is a power user; he's been using this tool every month, so he doesn't want to re-enter his departure address...perhaps we can save that for him? And then give him the ability to override?"

Understand How to Evaluate Designs

Many people who work in software, particularly those who come from a purely engineering or business background, are initially stymied when it comes to understanding UX design. Most team leads are not trained to be designers, nor do they want to be designers. And yet, the team lead is somehow responsible for ensuring that the user experience is "beautiful!"

Or "intuitive." Or, heaven forbid, "as good as the Apple iPhone launch." Yes, I've been in this latter category.

If you are responsible for shipping a great user experience, you must ask the Six UX Questions. You will also need to be reasonably thoughtful in your answers and make sure they make sense. If you do, you'll end up with a well-designed product. Remember to ask these questions every single time you review a set of mocks or designs.

THE SIX UX QUESTIONS

- What's the most important task the UI asks the user to accomplish?
- Is this the simplest solution?
- Is the information arranged logically?
- Is the design usable and discoverable?
- Are the standards consistent?
- Can you reduce the number of clicks or taps?

What's the most important task the UI asks your primary persona to accomplish?

When you approach a new user interface, you should start by asking yourself "what's the primary task our primary persona must accomplish?" and "what's the most important task the UI asks that persona to accomplish?" Focusing on your primary persona, instead of all your users, will help you prioritize better. If the answers to these questions are the same, you're in good shape. If they're not, you'll need to do some work. In some UIs, such as in a checkout workflow, these questions are simply answered. In other UIs, such as a home page for a baseball site, the question is much harder to answer. You can make the problem more manageable by talking through how your personas will experience the UI.

In the baseball example, you might say that both Paul the Power User and Chuck the Casual User want to know the latest scores. So let's organize the IA such that this information is most prominent. A third persona, Ellen the Emerging User, may want to focus on a favorite team. But since we know that Ellen is somewhat more motivated to customize her experience, our primary task is not to make the customization easy to perform from the home page. Instead, it's to make it easy for Ellen to *discover* the ability to customize. Similarly, since Paul the Power User has already specified a favorite team, we must give him a very quick way to log in or precustomize the UI since we recognize him.

In this example, it's important to clearly balance your goals and communicate them to your design team. If you're building an application for fantasy baseball players—whom you know from market research are pretty technical and want power tools—you'll tell your design team that the most important persona on which to focus is Paul the Power User, followed by Ellen the Emerging User, and lastly Chuck the Casual User, since he's probably getting his baseball information from ESPN anyway. However, if you're the *New York Times*, the vast majority of your users will likely be casual users like Chuck, and some substantial population will be from New York! Therefore, your priorities might be New York Casual Users, Other Casual Users, Emerging Users, and then Power Users.

It's important not to say, "Make the login button less prominent." We also didn't say, "Move the 'What's your favorite team?' promo up to the top." Rather, we empowered the design team to make a collection of optimizations based on our prioritized business objectives, which we clearly stated.

Another way to approach this is to ask direct questions, such as "Why is the login button in the middle of the screen?" If the designer says, "I wanted to make it really obvious!" you can say, "Mission accomplished! But our goal is to cater first to New York Casual Users—is that the right choice, given our prioritization of personas?" A good designer will be able to take this feedback and adjust the UI accordingly.

The design, business, and engineering teams must work closely together to define the priority of each persona. If you waffle or fail to communicate clear priorities, then the design team will grow frustrated and do your job for you, and you'll end up with a compromised user experience. Therefore, when you see a design for the first time, ask yourself these three questions:

- Who is the *most important user?*
- What is the *most important task* that the most important user must accomplish?
- Is the important user's important task *the most important and simplest element* in the UI?

The answers to the first two questions are business questions that set the context for the last question, which is a design question. If you find that your user has to go through a series of convoluted steps to accomplish the task, or has a hard time discovering how to start the task, then you want to stop where you are and redesign the UI. If your design team seems frustrated at this point, it's probably because you're asking them to juggle too many competing priorities, and you need to go back and answer questions one and two again.

Is this the simplest solution?

A user's ability to complete a task is a nonlinear function of its complexity. To restate for the less geeky reader: as you ask more from a user, the user's ability and willingness to do what you ask decreases. A lot. Ask yourself if your solution is the simplest possible solution to a user's problem. If the user wants to email an article about a baseball player to a friend, must the user create an account? Or can you enable the user to send the article as a courtesy and then upsell him or her to create an account? This latter approach is far more satisfying for users and saves a few substantial steps. It may also increase your abuse problems, so you need to make a smart product decision here. In this case, a good rule of thumb is to optimize for usability and solve the abuse problems when they become real. I've rarely seen this approach fail, and I have seen products stumble by trying to solve abuse problems that might never occur.

John Maeda proposes a framework for thinking about simplification in his book *The Laws of Simplicity* (MIT Press). He calls the framework SHE—*simplify, hide,* and *embody.* Similar to my previous suggestions, Maeda advocates "simplifying" features so they do only what they absolutely must. For advanced features that are used occasionally or by users of secondary importance, "hide" those more complicated features. One way to hide complexity is to put power-user features into an "advanced options" dialog or collapse them with a "zippy" arrow or +/– box, but remember that they must remain discoverable.

For features that can be transformed into something simpler, "embody" them with a parallel structure. For example, if you're trying to provide a color picker for shirts, you might be able to more simply embody the choice by showing pictures of each colored shirt, thereby eliminating the confusion a user would see in a text box drop-down that says "Color: Salmon." Is salmon pink or silver-blue? I guess it depends on whether you're a vegetarian.

Is the information organized logically?

In some cases, you need to balance the information you want to present with a call to action. The classic example is Amazon's product detail page. There's a tremendous amount of information on Amazon's pages, and the great beauty of them is that nearly every element is measured and sorted by how much money it makes. It is hard to measure the direct impact of some features, like customer reviews, and as a result, those features are at the bottom of the page! Other features are measured easily, such as the "What other items do customers buy after viewing this item," which is featured near the top of the product detail page.

In your case, you're unlikely to have such a simple-to-design (and hard-to-engineer) feature. You must think through the arrangement of your data and features logically. To arrange your data and features logically, you want to ensure that the following conditions are true:

- The most important information, for the most important customer type, is the most prominent.
- The information moves from headline to summary, just like a newspaper article.
- Wherever possible, information is personalized and real time. It's also good to provide as much detail as is reasonable. Why report "Sales rank: in the top 1000" when you can report "Sales rank: 1327"? Users appreciate precision, within limits.
- The most frequently used controls are the easiest to access.

Is the design usable and discoverable?

After you've identified the core tasks that users want to perform, you should ask yourself if those tasks are discoverable and understandable. *Discoverability* speaks to the ability of a user to find the call to action, such as "Add to Cart." If your users have a hard time discovering the "Add to Cart" button, your career will be short-lived. Similarly, what if the "Add to Cart" button is actually a plus sign in a button and you were at the helm? That design fails the understandability test, so you're probably fired.

There are many ways to solve discovery problems. Here are three common solutions you can try:

Positioning

The priority of information starts at the top left and descends to the lower right in Western cultures. If you want to place your call to action in the most obvious place, you probably want to put it on the top left of your content.

There are key exceptions to this rule, however. One exception is "banner blindness," wherein users have become so used to "punch the monkey" ads in the top center of their browser that they ignore any content located there. Similarly, many websites use a left-justified navigation scheme, and any context-based call to action placed there will likely be lost.

You may hear designers say that a visual element is "below the fold." This is an old print expression that means some story is on the bottom half of the newspaper page, or "below the fold" and therefore not visible on the newsstand. In web browser terms, the "fold" is located where the browser ends on a common screen, about 600 px from the top. iPads, Androids, and other devices have different folds based on their screen resolution. If an item is below the fold, its discoverability drops dramatically.

Visual design

Making your call to action prominent by adjusting size, using color strategically, or breaking the grid can go a long way toward solving discovery problems. Unfortunately, visual design can also create major problems. One of the best ways to make things pretty is to simplify and streamline them, like shaving the door handles off a car. The car looks pretty, but you can't open the door. Beware of very slick visual affordances that cripple usability and discoverability.

Conventions

Applications, sites, and businesses all rely on a design language to make tasks understandable. For example, the streets on Google Maps are white and yellow, just as they are in cartography. If your designer were to make lakes white, chaos would ensue. Similarly, if you were to reverse the positions of the OK and Cancel buttons in your dialogs willy-nilly, users would constantly click the wrong button. You can make your software much better by asking the design team to articulate conventions and then checking to make sure they follow the conventions.

If you have questions about the discoverability or usability of a feature, one of the best ways to test is on real users. Usability tests can expose whether users see your call to action. In addition, placing metrics on click targets through tools like Google Analytics can measure conversion, and running A/B comparison experiments will help you understand which designs work best.

Are the standards consistent?

Leveraging conventions gives you design shorthand that enables users to almost skip ahead in your UI. For example, on Mac interfaces, the OK button is always on the lower-right side of a UI, so users can click the button without having to read the copy above the button or read the name of the button. Sadly, PCs are different, and the OK button appears to the left of the Cancel button on the bottom-right side. If you're building a web application, this convention doesn't help. But you'd best make sure that within your application the buttons are in a consistent place, especially if you're working in iOS or Android.

Here are some other conventions you can leverage to make your UI more understandable:

- Make all primary buttons large and the same color.
- Have only one primary button in a UI.
- Use multiple buttons for choices like yes or no.
- Use a different style for primary, secondary, and tertiary calls to action. For example, on Amazon.com there's a "Buy Now" button (the primary action, we can only hope) and lots of little "Learn more" links (the secondary action). Amazon's system works well because buttons are more obvious than links and because Amazon maintains this convention throughout the site, all the way to the "Your Account" section.
- For three or more pages in a workflow, show what step the user is in and the total number of steps.
- Use underlines or a color that strongly diverges from the text in your application for links.
- Follow Internet standards for CSS (e.g., mouseover on a link should change the pointer to a hand).

Can you reduce the number of clicks?

Now that you've addressed the general workflow a user experiences, try to reduce the number of clicks. You might ask yourself if you can combine a form that's two pages into one page, for example. The number of clicks a user must make has such a strong impact on the user's ability to complete a task that Amazon holds a patent on "1-Click" buying (US PAT NO. 5960411).

You should also carefully consider the default settings for user options. If your defaults are correct, users will click fewer times and experience fewer unexpected consequences. Designers typically refer to checkboxes that are checked by default as "opt-out" and checkboxes that are unchecked as "opt-in."

Another important aspect of reducing clicks is reducing the number of times that a user switches from the keyboard to the mouse and vice versa. There is a substantial cost to users each time they must reacquire the mouse and its pointer. Do your best to eliminate these switching events.

Understand How to Communicate with Designers

Designers have a hard job because everyone has an opinion about design. As a result, designers are rarely treated like experts. If you treat them like the experts they are, however, and focus on asking the right questions, you can drive very high-quality design and help designers own their work. That said, people work in different ways, and designers are people. Some designers are more sensitive than others and some are more tolerant than others. Some designers may want to hear "it feels crowded," while others may want to slug you if you say that. Adopt and modify the following communication tips for your unique designer:

Use the user's voice

Start feedback with the words, "As a [user type] I want to..." This approach works so well that the Scrum approach to project management uses this format to create "user stories" to which developers code.

Ask questions to drive understanding

For example, you might ask, "What is the convention for a back button on iOS? Is this consistent?" Your goal should not be to dictate a specific experience, but rather to get to an agreement on design rationale that will inform specific designs that your team will create.

Reiterate business goals and relative priority of conflicting goals

Help your designer understand the problem that he or she must solve. Designers make a thousand judgment calls per day, and they use extensive experience to make great optimizations. You can help guide their decision making by ensuring that they understand your goals. Make your goals concrete. For example: "Most users should not need to scroll. Therefore, we should try to keep input fields above the fold, right?"

You can also help your team by not setting subjective goals. Goals like "Users must feel at home in the app" or "It needs to feel friendlier" make me cringe. How do you know you've achieved these goals?

When a usability participant shows up and takes a nap? Instead, look for the root cause of your design problem. For example: "We're asking users to pay $10 on the home page before they see any value. Let's come up with an experience that lets users understand what we have to offer before we ask for their credit card!"

Be quantitative

You can count clicks, screens, and page load time to make conversations concrete. Embrace usability testing. Similarly, avoid saying things that are subjective, like sentences that start with "This feels..." or "I like..."

Provide examples from competitors or similar experiences that work well

Dissecting competitive experiences with your designer will help you create a collective design language. You can also ask your user experience researcher to review competitive products and analyze the industry's best practices.

Learn How to Communicate with Pictures

Mockups come in a few different flavors. One of the most simple and powerful tools is a whiteboard drawing. When you find your designer staring blankly at you like you're speaking Klingon, turn to the whiteboard and draw a picture. You can go one step further and clean the picture up a bit and take a picture with your cell phone. These cell phone and whiteboard drawings are remarkably powerful as a communication tool and are simple to make. I've seen teams like the style of these drawings so much that they build animated videos out of collections of photos.

The simplest form of formal mockups are grayscale *wireframes* that show the structure of your app and emphasize the text and layout but not the visual design. *Comps,* or more refined visual mocks, are useful for understanding the visual weight of elements and provide a great specification for your team, especially when they are turned into *redlines.* Redlines are just detailed mocks with red callouts that specify the size and color of elements. The final major type of mock is the *clickable prototype,* which is an extension of the wireframe and the most expensive mock to build. Clickable prototypes are incredibly useful because you can give them to users in usability studies and see how users actually experience your product.

When I need to use mocks to communicate an idea in a document or presentation, I start with wireframes because they're the simplest form of mocks. If you add too much detail, such as colors, images, and other flourishes, you'll find that some of the people who review your mocks will get lost in the details. When making wireframes, focus on these basics:

- Mock up only the relevant parts of the UI.
- Always use the full, properly edited text.
- Limit the amount of time you spend on visual design.
- Use grayscale, not color.
- Assume that your wireframes will change a lot.
- Watch out for cheats.

Mock up only the relevant parts of the UI
For example, you can start with a full web page and then show just a dialog box and a snippet of an email confirmation. The advantage of this approach is that it saves you time, avoids creating details that are inconsistent, and eliminates duplication that you'll have to adjust many times later.

Always use the full, properly edited text
Text, or "copy," is incredibly useful for explaining what the intent of the interface is. You can use the Latin *Lorem ipsum* filler that designers use if you have blocks of placeholder text, but for any forms, buttons, dialogs, or other meaningful controls, you really must use ship-quality copy. This copy will help your team understand precisely what various elements of the UI are supposed to do. Copy is also your canary in a coal mine; if you find that you have to write a paragraph to explain how a feature works, you should redesign the feature because users don't read paragraphs of instructions.

Limit the time you spend on visual design
Visual design, branding, naming, and other elements are subjective. They are also rarely focused on enabling the user to complete a task. Unlike copy, these fancy elements don't help you understand the user experience, and if you do add them they will likely create style-focused discussions that are unrelated to the problem you're trying to solve. Instead, put clearly labeled placeholder boxes where these visual elements will go, and then move on.

Use grayscale, not color

For the most part, color will overcomplicate your wireframes and raise questions of visual design and branding. See the preceding wireframe tip.

Assume that your wireframes will change a lot

Wireframes are great for quickly communicating an idea and promoting discussion. When you reach consensus, your design team will build high-fidelity mocks, but until then your wireframes will change a lot. Therefore, wireframes should be made in such a way that you can modify them quickly. Don't worry when people tear your wireframes apart, because that means you're doing a good job driving the conversation forward.

Watch out for cheats!

It's easy to cheat when you're pushing pixels, not code. For example, rounding corners or adding transparency tends to make things look slick. It's easy to forget to include opt-out checkboxes and legal copy that the lawyers say you have to show. And it's easy to pretend that the user has tons of personal information that make pages or interfaces look rich and full. Be wary of these traps. Consider both the new user and the experienced user when you build these mocks, and make sure that what you're building isn't using visual tricks that you can't actually deliver.

If you're lucky enough to have a designer build mocks with you, then you might not need to know how to make them. Knowing the basics of wireframes will help you have empathy, and that's probably good enough. But most leaders in the software industry need to draw a picture at some point, and designers have developed some nice ways of making simple pictures quickly that you might benefit from. There are two simple processes that most designers use. The first is using a flowcharting program like Visio or Omnigraffle to make wireframes, and the second is using Fireworks, Photoshop, or Paint to make small, near-pixel-perfect changes to existing UIs. Both of these techniques are great to know, so we'll cover them next.

CREATE SIMPLE WIREFRAMES IN OMNIGRAFFLE

I make wireframes in Omnigraffle. It is a fantastic program, and you will learn a lot about design just by working in it since its creators made so many good decisions about how to use the software. You can perform similar operations in Visio, but it lacks some of Omnigraffle's nice features.

If you're going to build a series of slides for a linear walkthrough of the user experience, you probably want to use *layers*. Layers are like pieces of tracing paper that can be displayed, hidden, or overlaid any which way. They enable you to create the common elements, like an image of an empty browser, as a layer that you can put on the bottom of your stack. By doing so, that empty browser will show through all the other layers and make your wireframes look like they're in a web browser. You'll want to "lock" that layer so you don't accidentally edit it while you're working on another layer. In Figure 3-1, I've created a browser template with my title and locked it.

Figure 3-1. Creating layers in Omnigraffle

Next, create layers for each slide you're going to show. In other words, create a layer for each click or step in the UX.

At this point, you have a basic wireframe template that you can easily modify. Now, say you want to extend this template to make it more easily modifiable, such as by adding a common header. To do so, just make a new layer, and position it at the top of all the other layers so it overlays the other steps (Figure 3-2). Then, lock it to make subsequent edits easier.

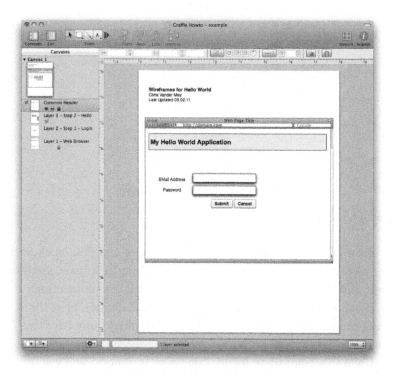

Figure 3-2. Making a common header in Omnigraffle

Now you're ready to make your individual pages. One of the things that makes Omnigraffle great for making wireframes is the stencil feature. (Visio has a similar feature.) Stencils, shown in Figure 3-3, are editable stamps that allow you to drag and drop UI elements into your wireframes. I use a wonderful library of wireframe stencils from Konigi; the library contains just about everything you'd ever need. You can find it here: *http://konigi.com/tools/omnigraffle-wireframe-stencils.*

Figure 3-3. Omnigraffle stencils, showing buttons

Turn off the visibility of all unlocked layers and then click on the layer that represents the step you want to edit. Drag in buttons, text boxes, labels, and other elements from your stencil to make your wireframe.

If you need to add notes, you can use red callouts—or redlines, as mentioned earlier—to point to the things you want to annotate. This feature works well, doesn't it?

Up to this point we've focused on linear workflows, and you've been able to create slides for a presentation. But users frequently have different ways to approach a given task, and there are error states that you need to account for. In cases like these, you can build your wireframes more like a flowchart.

To make a wireframe-based flowchart, draw the first wireframe, just as you did previously, but don't worry about layers. See Figure 3-4 for a simple example of a Hello World application.

Next, add the second step, connect the two images with lines, and put the step number on it (Figure 3-5). You'll probably want to add comments to explain what happens.

Figure 3-4. Flowchart wireframes, step 1: drawing the first wireframe

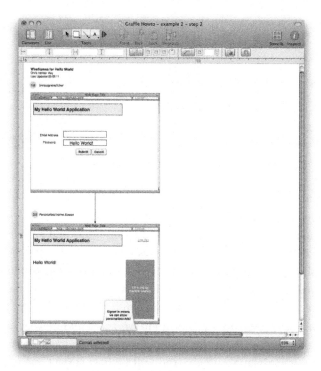

Figure 3-5. Flowchart wireframes, step 2: connecting the images

Here's a nice optimization: for the third step, you can make a dialog instead of building the whole UI again (see Figure 3-6).

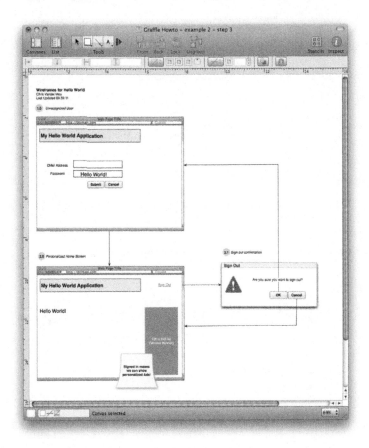

Figure 3-6. Flowchart wireframes, step 3: making a dialog and completing the flowchart

Omnigraffle is a powerful tool, and using boxes and simple text elements makes absorbing design changes easy. If you want to build even more sophisticated mocks, you can create referenced components as objects to make changes even quicker to apply. You can set properties and scripts on objects to create clickable mockups for tests. You can do many of the same operations in Visio or in Fireworks—and Fireworks will even export production-ready art for you. But your goal is to communicate requirements clearly and quickly. You will be best served leaving the advanced tools to the designers and keeping your mocks simple.

MAKE PRODUCTION-QUALITY MOCKS QUICKLY

Sometimes wireframes won't cut it, though. Perhaps the change is so small that making wireframes seems too complicated. Or perhaps you really do need to be extremely clear about a focused change to some feature. For these kinds of changes, I prefer to use Photoshop, Fireworks, or another image editor because I get a higher-fidelity representation with less work than I would in Omnigraffle. Luckily, you don't need to be a Photoshop or Fireworks wizard to build simple, high-fidelity mocks quickly.

Let's say we want to list our Hello World application underneath the Kindle heading on Amazon's home page. You would start by taking a screenshot of the UI you need to change. Open it in your program (in these examples, Fireworks) and resize the canvas to give you space to work.

Using the marquee tool, cut out the part you need to change or make space for your addition. I cut and moved the part down the page because I intend to insert a new option (Option-Shift-drag on the marquee); see Figure 3-7.

Figure 3-7. Cut the page apart

Copy the basic element you need using the marquee and Command-Option-dragging. In this case, I'll use the Kindle entry. Paste it in, then delete and fill in the Kindle-specific space and other areas with the appropriate background. (See Figure 3-8.) One trick you can use is to keep using the marquee tool to copy and paste the background color from another area to do the filling, rather than trying to use the paint bucket and eraser.

Figure 3-8. Copy and paste the basic element

Add your element. As shown in Figure 3-9, I'm adding my Hello World with a green "NEW!" prompt. You won't do anything quite so stupid. (Jeff would never approve.) I guessed at the font, but you'll probably know what your production fonts are. Or you can inspect the CSS!

Figure 3-9. Add your specific details

Clean up the bottom and crop the image back down to the basic size. Done! (See Figure 3-10.)

Figure 3-10. Finished mock in Fireworks

This example is trivial, but you'll find that you can generate a remarkable number of high-quality mocks in a short period of time using this technique.

4

How to Achieve Project Management Greatness on a Budget

As your product development continues, you'll need to stay on top of your project so that you can coordinate with other teams, plan the launch, and ensure that your dependencies are met. You need to handle this level of project management while also doing everything else. Unfortunately for your team, but fortunately for your paycheck, your time is at a premium. A team lead can rarely afford to build and maintain a sophisticated project model in Microsoft Project, and you will probably not be able to bring in part-time talent to work the night shift and "crash" the project (meaning, complete it in less time). If you want to be great at shipping software, you need bargain-basement project management.

I think understanding project management is sufficiently important that I ask about it during phone screen interviews for product managers. I ask, "How do you know if your product is going to ship on time?" To be fair, this is a trick question since nobody ever really knows if the product will ship on time. But you can estimate. A great answer to my question involves three low-cost tasks:

1. Build and maintain a simple schedule.
2. Track your bugs, watch your burndown, and calculate your *zero bug bounce* (ZBB) date.
3. Manage your dependencies carefully.

These three cheap tasks apply to waterfall or agile development processes. Each team you work with will want to manage their project differently, but these three tasks are generally applicable. If you learn how to do them well and quickly, you'll be in great shape. Worst case, you'll know that you need to change something!

Build and Maintain a Simple Schedule

You need to have a schedule, because if you don't, you'll have no idea if you can ship. A simple schedule doesn't need much more than a list of tasks and engineering estimates of how much time an engineer or designer needs to complete each task. All you need to do is sort these tasks according to the priority of the features they support and allocate the tasks across your team, and you've got a schedule. It doesn't need to be any more complicated than that.

It is easy to do more project management than you need. You can go crazy with feature backlogs in an agile process, or you can use software like Microsoft Project. After years of fussing with these systems, I've learned that my teams and I prefer to use a simple Google spreadsheet that accumulates these tasks and estimates. The spreadsheet I've developed does everything that you really need. And, in addition to being free, your whole team can edit it in real time! You can find a working example at *www.shippinggreatness.com*. Figure 4-1 shows what it looks like.

	A	E	F	G	H
8	Today's Date:		3/2/2012	(replace with =Today() to get current projections)	
9	Buffer Assumption:		0.6		
10	Days Code/Days Test		3		
11	Push assumption		Tuesday or Thursday (2, 4)		
12					
13					
14	**Release dates**				
15	Version	Code Complete	Test Complete	Push Complete	
16	V1	3/17	3/22	3/27	
17	V2	3/26	3/31	4/5	
18	V3	4/9	4/14	4/19	
19					
20	**Task Allocation**				
21	Teammate	V1	V2	V3	etc
22	chris@domain.com	6	4	0	
23	viki@domain.com	2	0	5	
24					
25	**Task Breakdown**				
26	Task	Time remaining (D)	Target Version (or milestone)	Assigned Engineer	Dependencies
27	Chris's Vacation	5		V1 chris@domain.com	
28	Email sending	1		V1 chris@domain.com	post-vacation
29	Email formatting	2		V1 viki@domain.com	
30	Customize email content	4		V2 chris@domain.com	
31	Feedback form	5		V3 viki@domain.com	
32					

Figure 4-1. Sample project management spreadsheet

Here's how this spreadsheet works. You can download it from *www.shippinggreatness.com* and follow along if you want. In partnership with your development lead, start by entering the tasks into the Task

Breakdown section. Enter planned vacations as tasks (they're not account-ed for in the buffer). Next, for each task, estimate the time remaining in unbuffered developer days and make a guess about which engineer can do the work. Assign each task a target version of the product. You may know these versions as "iterations," but they're the same thing—your releases. The remaining data you must enter are your assumptions about buffer and approximately how much testing you need (e.g., for each three days of development, you need one day of your test team to test). The testing con-stant is a function of the size of your test team. In the spreadsheet shown in Figure 4-1, I've added some calculations to ensure that tasks don't end on the weekends.

Because this model uses "ideal" developer days for estimates, it is criti-cal to build a buffer into your dates, but not the engineering task estimates. A buffer is a "fudge factor" that accommodates unforeseen problems and general productivity losses. Some teams estimate that approximately three out of five days are productive. Anything could be happening in those two days, but it's likely some combination of meetings, broken builds, marriage problems, and false starts. It's pretty hard to eliminate those distractions, and as a result I find that 60% productivity is a good estimate. If you have systems in production, however, you may be even less efficient since you have to maintain them and serve existing customers. Early-stage projects are more efficient because there aren't bugs to fix yet. An impor-tant thing to note is that the 60% buffer assumes bug fixing time and unplanned personal days, but not vacations.

I also added a "Push assumption" field to this spreadsheet because it's good advice not to push new software to your servers on a Friday. You don't want to be the guy desperately trying to extract your inebriated en-gineering team from a bar at midnight so you can patch a privacy breach! In other cases, teams want regular release days because they have kindly operations folks who help with pushes. In this case, I assumed the team would push only on Tuesdays and Thursdays.

Now your data entry is complete, and you're almost done. Next, you and your development lead must balance the tasks and adjust the versions to fit your dates. Look at the task allocation section and find the engineer with the most work remaining. This engineer is sometimes referred to as "the long pole" or "on the critical path." Try to assign some of his or her tasks for the V1 release to another engineer who is not fully allocated. If you do this right, you will have balanced the tasks across your engineering team, and each engineer will have nearly the same amount of work to do.

Now that you have a balanced plan, you may want to look at your release dates. If V1 seems like it's too far out and you want to push for a faster initial release, or if you want to ensure that you have a release every two weeks, you can move some tasks from V1 to V2. Move the least important tasks in V1 into V2 by changing the values in the Task Breakdown section, and rebalance the task allocation across the team. Check your release dates for holidays and against critical team outages; if everything looks good, you're done.

I like this spreadsheet for a lot of reasons:

- I created it. Never discount pride of authorship...
- Your team can easily update their time remaining and see how the project is going. They can also add tasks as they discover them, because it's a collaborative spreadsheet in Google Docs.
- It's easy to see the long pole.
- It's easy to configure or customize.
- It's easy to track vacations because you add vacations as tasks.
- It's easy to push tasks into further versions if you aren't making your date by changing the "target version" to which a task is targeted. You can also use this model for tracking milestones.
- It works just fine for 30-day sprints.
- It's easy to balance tasks across the team. If you don't want Chris on the critical path for V1, reassign his tasks to Viki.
- It forecasts your dates well, including code complete, test complete, and push complete. Now your test team knows when they should plan to start a new test pass, and your marketing team knows when customers will see the product.
- It communicates your assumptions up front for the team.
- A day is the right unit of measurement for tracking tasks. You can always use "0.2" days for really small tasks, but I find that extra-small tasks are best tracked in bugs.

While this spreadsheet doesn't have neat features like integrating with a bug tracking system or a source repository, its only major drawback is that it doesn't track dependencies. I've learned to handle that problem through comments beside the line-item tasks and through discussions with the team during our daily standup meetings.

When all the major work on a project is done and the team is almost exclusively fixing bugs, I stop using the schedule. Instead, I use the bug list and a bug burndown chart. We'll cover how to build and use a bug burndown shortly.

HOW TO GET ESTIMATES

Some managers find asking engineers for estimates uncomfortable. What's more, some engineers underestimate and others overestimate. You won't know who errs in which direction until you've worked with the team for a while. To make estimates easier to get and less costly for the engineering team to produce, try the following techniques:

If you're not an engineering manager, ask your engineering manager to get the estimates
  'Nuff said.

Accept the estimates at face value
  If an estimate is very large (greater than a week), ask the engineer to break that down into smaller tasks. Beyond that, complain to your engineering manager.

Feel entitled
  If you are an engineering manager, estimates are something to which you are entitled. You made a commitment to support your team, and they need to make a similar commitment to support the project. It's only fair. Feel free to remind your team that you made this commitment to them, as long as you stand by it.

Track only time remaining
  I track only the time that remains on a task, not the percentage of the task that is completed or the estimated amount of time a task will take versus the actual amount of time it took. The estimated-time-versus-actual-time metric provides no real insight beyond identifying who is a good estimator, and you're going to learn that anyway. You'll also find that less experienced engineers almost always underestimate while more experienced engineers overestimate, so you can use that rule of thumb instead of tracking the estimated and actual times.

  Tracking only the time remaining to complete a task is an agile tenet that I like because it emphasizes the reality of the project and makes it easy to see when you're going to hit the code complete date.

Ask for nonbuffered estimates

You can build in buffer in your spreadsheet and make it visible so that the team knows you are compensating for problems that might (will!) arise. I see lots of religious arguments around this topic, but this approach is the cleanest I've seen.

Update the time remaining estimates in a team meeting once per week

Updating your estimates as a team on a weekly basis prevents you from harassing your team and allows teammates to provide context on why things are moving quicker or slower than expected. This process also helps identify if someone is going to be blocked.

Track Your Bugs and Build a Bug Burndown

A bug burndown chart displays your bug count versus time as a graph. You'll use it to predict when you can ship. To make one, plot curves for each level of bug severity versus time. You will also want to plot a curve for the total number of bugs versus time. You can see a sample bug burndown chart in Figure 4-2.

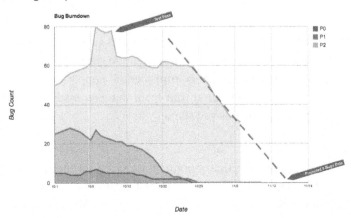

Figure 4-2. Sample bug burndown

You should expect that your bug count will go up and to the right as you get nearer to code complete, and then down and to the right as you get closer to launch. The rate at which these bugs decline, or the slope of that line, is called the *find/fix ratio*. You can't accurately predict your date without sizing individual bugs until you are fixing more bugs than you are finding, which means your find/fix ratio will be less than 1.

When your find/fix drops below 1, you can forecast when you'll ship at a given quality level by projecting the date at which the bug count hits zero. In Figure 4-2, you'll see that we can reasonably say we'll have fixed all super-critical bugs for our "dogfood" release by October 31 and that we could ship around November 15. If you don't like the date you calculate, you have only two options. You can change your quality bar, or you can add engineering talent to fix more bugs more quickly.

Managing Dependencies

There's no secret recipe for managing dependencies. All you can do is minimize your risk. There are a few key tools you can use to minimize the risk that your dependencies introduce. I call them the "Five Ifs."

If you can live without it, live without it
> It should be self-evident that if you need to accomplish less, you will have less risk. Removing features will always reduce your risk. In early versions of your product, you can cut risk by replacing features with manual labor. For example, instead of making a customer support request form, add a customer support email address as a *mailto:* link. Sure, it'll take more work to resolve contacts, but you probably don't know how many contacts you'll have yet, so postpone that investment and cut the risk.

If you can build it in-house, build it in-house
> Some of the most effective teams at Google—Android and Chrome in particular—are emphatic about following the "build everything in-house" approach. They allow virtually nothing to be built outside their teams, and while this can frustrate others and slow down development in some areas, it has created an environment that enables them to ship frequently. It's hard to argue with shipping!

If you must take a dependency, take it early
> By tackling your riskiest problems first, you'll be able to take the appropriate corrective action sooner and increase your confidence in your final ship date.

*If you must take dependencies, depend on the previous version that's
already built*

It's always tempting to say, "Version 2 of the Foo service will be so
much easier for us to work with—and the Foo Version 2 team is
making good progress! Let's plan on using V2, since V1 is really ugly."
This approach is almost always a false economy. Risk is the enemy of
shipping.

If you ship early, you are less likely to be damaged by your dependencies

This principle is counterintuitive but useful. Systems and products
that you plan to work with change underneath you all the time. For
example, a beneficial business relationship you were depending on
could be invalidated when the partner hires a new CEO—and your
ability to predict such an event is nil. Therefore, shipping early and
often helps reduce risk.

5

How to Do a Great Job Testing

IF YOUR SOFTWARE DOESN'T work, you won't sell it. Worse, you'll be embarrassed by it. This is why I apply the High School Embarrassment Test (HSET™) to any product I want to ship. The HSET works because high school did deep psychological damage to most of us and left behind hormone-based scars that industries like Hollywood have mined to great effect. You can leverage these scars as well. All you need to do is ask yourself: am I sure I won't be embarrassed when an old high school friend sees my product? That's all there is to the HSET.

The HSET helps ensure that your team is happy. Tom DeMarco and Timothy Lister point out in their book *Peopleware: Productive Projects and Teams* (Dorset House) that one of the best ways to destroy your team is to ask them to ship something they aren't proud of. Remember, your engineering team members have old high school buddies too. You need to ensure that your team isn't embarrassed.

So, how do you ensure that the software you ship does not embarrass you? There are eight major steps you can take that will have a substantial impact on the quality of your shipping product:

1. Insist on test-driven development.
2. Build a testing team around a great test lead.
3. Review your test plan and test cases personally.
4. Automate testing.
5. Dogfood religiously.
6. Have a big bug bash.
7. Triage your bugs diligently.
8. Establish trusted testers as a last line of defense.

If you do these eight things, you'll be well on your way to shipping a great product. Let's dig into how to do them.

Insist on Test-Driven Development

There's an expression routinely vouchsafed in advertisements posted on Google's restroom walls that reads "Debugging sucks. Testing rocks." This mantra is powerful. Debugging requires you to deconstruct and disassemble your software until you get to the point where you find the problem. That's effectively moving backward. Moving backward is the opposite of shipping. In addition to helping you feel confident that you're doing the right thing, test-driven development helps your team survive in complicated systems environments, because as soon as another engineer or team breaks an interface you depend on, the tests will fail.

Test-driven development is covered extensively in other references (see Appendix C), but here's an overview of the process:

1. Eddie Engineer breaks the work down into pieces that perform simple operations. These are called units. For example, countToTen() is a software unit.
2. Before Eddie writes the countToTen method, he writes a test—known as a *unit test*. This basically says, "If countToTen() is equal to 10, then pass; else, fail."
3. Now that Eddie has the unit test written, he can write the countToTen method. If Eddie's index is off on the loop and countToTen() actually outputs 9, the test will fail.
4. When the software builds, all the unit tests are run automatically.

Pretty straightforward, right? It is. It takes some discipline, though. What's extra-great about test-driven development is that regressions are easier to spot because each build runs tests automatically. Look into software like JUnit (for Java-based unit testing) to automate your build and verification procedures.

Build a Test Team Around a Test Lead

No matter how good your engineering team is and regardless of how many unit tests they have written, you will have bugs. Your best plan of action to find these bugs is to hire or appoint someone to be the test guru. This test lead will be the primary owner of release quality and a critical partner to product management, engineering, and marketing leads. Test leads are responsible for making sure that the test cases are well written, cover the right areas, and are well executed. A great test lead will continuously train less experienced testers and help design great test automation architecture. If you have a really strong test lead, that individual will be sharp enough to push the engineering team to build more and better unit tests.

Another key reason why you want to start with a great test lead is that the test team culture is frequently unlike the engineering team culture. Your test team is trying to discover problems all day long. In a typical but poorly run engineering team, the test team generates complaints daily, and that can be hard to take. The processes, disciplines, and standards are a bit different than typical engineering teams, so having a solid test lead who can help manage the test team will help you immensely, even if you've done a great job of embedding testing with engineering.

Your test lead will also help you solve the unique problem of hiring testers. Brilliant test engineers are hard to come by because most folks who can write great software want to write their own software, not test the software your engineering team wrote. There are two ways to extract yourself from this dilemma: maintain a lower hiring bar and hire managers, or maintain a high hiring bar and hire contractors. As I'll describe next, there are advantages to both approaches, but I favor hiring contractors.

OPTION 1: MAINTAIN A LOWER HIRING BAR, AND HIRE MANAGERS

I'm not a fan of hiring managers to hire test engineers who are not rock stars. I believe the practice establishes the wrong incentives. It builds in hierarchy, and your talented test manager has to spend a substantial portion of his or her time managing nonstellar performers. However, the opportunity to manage people is a strong incentive for some individuals.

What's even worse about maintaining a lower hiring bar is that eventually you're going to have to promote some of these folks. After five years, they're going to feel entitled to a promotion and you'll be in a situation where you've got B-level people in management. Unfortunately, the expression "As hire As, Bs hire Cs" is definitely true in the software industry. When you hit this stage of corporate maturity, your productivity and quality will sharply decline as a result of your C-grade players.

OPTION 2: MAINTAIN A HIGH HIRING BAR, AND WORK WITH VENDOR TESTERS

There are some disadvantages to working with contracted testers. These disadvantages include:

- You need a development lead to own the relationship with the testers. For this reason, embedding contractors within a team adds overhead to your engineering team.
- Training costs are sunk and irretrievable.
- Your ramped-up test talents' contracts can expire, and they might take their knowledge elsewhere.

In my opinion, the advantages of contracted testers outweigh the disadvantages. Some of the advantages include:

- Contractors cost the organization less in terms of people management than full-time hires do.
- It is easier to engage with an agency than it is to hire, so you can ramp up faster. And you can maintain a consistent quality bar.
- You don't promote the C-grade players.

OPTION 3: MAINTAIN A HIGH HIRING BAR, AND DON'T USE CONTRACTORS

This is not an option. Google tried this. It just doesn't work, and one of two things happened every time: bugs shipped, or engineers did the testing. And more often than not, folks ended up embarrassed. Use this approach at your peril.

Review Your Test Plan and Test Cases

Regardless of how you build your test team, you still need someone to write a test plan and you need to ensure the quality of the test cases, which means you need to review and approve the test plan.

A test plan is composed of many test cases and is derived from your product requirements document. It is therefore reasonable to expect that if your product requirements document stinks, your testing team is set up for failure. But if you did your job well, then your test lead can do a great job too.

The test plan is generally created in a spreadsheet so you can organize the test cases well. Check to see that your test cases have the following descriptive elements:

Area of focus
This column describes what part of the user experience will be tested, so you can group similar tests together.

Severity
The severity defines what level of bug you should file if this test fails, generally on a scale of 1–4.

Preconditions
Preconditions establish what the tester must do before starting the test. For example, if you were writing a test for a shopping cart credit card verification process, the preconditions might require that the user be logged in, have added an item to the cart, and have entered a zip code. Now the test can start.

Tasks to perform
The tasks are the meat of the test, described as a series of steps. If any step fails, the test will fail.

Post-conditions
The post-conditions describe the final state of the application. To continue the example, the post-conditions might be that the user sees a confirmation page with a confirmation number, and the credit card is charged the correct amount in less than 10 seconds.

Figure 5-1 shows an example test case.

	A	B	C	D	E
1	Area of Focus	Severity	Pre-Conditions	Tasks	Post-Conditions
2	Animal Upload	S1	User is logged in	1. Navigate to home page 2. Click "Upload Animal" 3. Attach "//src/giraffe.jpg" 4. Submit	1. User is redirected to animal detail page. 2. Animal detail page shows the giraffe.

Figure 5-1. Test case spreadsheet

Because you've included the "severity" of each test, you can create quicker but less complete test passes by running only the high-priority tests. Test passes like these are good for verifying small changes. You can test only the small change and the high-severity tests in much less time than running all the tests. It's important to still run the high-severity tests, even if you think the small change is well isolated from other features. You want to make sure that some fundamental feature wasn't accidentally turned off. In a complicated software system with weak unit testing, it is easy to break major features—and the HSET preaches a "better safe than very sorry" approach.

The output of a full test pass is bugs and sometimes a sense of surprise. This is a great moment for you, as the team lead, to reinforce a "bad news is good news" mantra and greet the number of bugs found by the test team with loud applause. Think about it: you need the test team motivated to find failures. If your team ends up demoralized each time there's a test pass, or if the relationship between test and development becomes acrimonious, you're going to end up with fewer bugs and—wait for it—embarrassment!

Reviewing test cases can be incredibly boring. You need to do it nevertheless, if only to empathize with your test team. Here's a trick: instead of slogging through *all* of your test cases, which is ideal and will get you a round of applause from anyone who notices, focus on the following three things:

User experience
> Make sure that there are cases that cover vital parts of the user experience, especially the "getting started" workflows and error cases.

Security and privacy
> Tests should try to break your website.

Dependencies
> If you rely on a database, third-party service, or software you didn't build in-house, make sure those dependencies are tested rigorously. They're likely to break or change without notice.

If your test plan covers these major areas, you're starting from a good place.

Automate Testing

Remember how hard it is to hire a great test lead? One of the best workarounds for this challenge is to find a test lead who's willing to write test automation. If your test lead is able to craft testing systems that work independently from your production code, you've created a great project for a test engineer. What's more, that software can run constantly and do the work of dozens of people.

You may be thinking, "Wait—that's a lot of extra software to write!" Luckily, most test automation can be written in scripting languages, doesn't need to scale particularly well, and can use established, pre-existing frameworks. Test development can therefore be more efficient.

As a team lead you probably don't need to own test automation, but you do need to make sure that it's being built, because while you'll never be able to afford enough testers, you will be able to afford enough computers on which to run the automation.

Dogfood

Microsoft pioneered the notion of "eating your own dogfood," which means you should use the software you intend to ship within your company. Put another way, don't feed your team peoplefood but give your customers dogfood. Forcing you and your team to suffer through customer pain is a great way to instill a sense of urgency, understand customer problems, and find defects. Amazon and Google dogfood religiously.

Dogfooding can be challenging when there's a good alternative, such as the prior, less buggy version of your software. For example, Google wanted employees to dogfood Google Docs, and the best way to force that issue was to stop installing Microsoft Office on corporate computers by default. In addition to driving dogfood of Google Docs, the practice saved money!

In some cases, making it easier to taste the dogfood also works. For example, Amazon wanted employees to dogfood Amazon Prime, so they made it available to employees at a discount. I've seen teams offer awards (from t-shirts to iPads) for the most unique bugs reported. I even saw one engineering director offer a $5,000 bounty for a successful series of steps to reproduce a "heisenbug." A heisenbug is a bug that spuriously appears and disappears, following the Heisenberg uncertainty principle;[1] they're a pain in the ass. However you do it, make dogfooding a key part of your team culture even if the other teams you work with don't do it.

---

1   *http://en.wikipedia.org/wiki/Uncertainty_principle*

One fun part of the dogfood experience is that you'll find your CEO always has some kind of awful experience that nobody else has seen. The first time this happens to you, you'll be chagrined. This was precisely the person you wanted to impress, and you botched it! Forgive yourself now, because soon you'll understand that every team lead has the same experience. Jeff Bezos always finds bizarre bugs. Things always break on Larry Page's computer. There are many examples of these failures, and one pretty common reason for them: these execs are awesome dogfooders.

In Larry's case, he has more alpha software on his computer and more experiments running on his account than you could possibly imagine, because team leads like you are desperate to convince Larry that they are making progress. It's no surprise that there are bizarre interactions. Your best defense in Larry's case is to figure out what else could interact with your product and plan for it.

In Jeff's case, he brings a completely fresh perspective to your product because he's never seen it before and has no idea what he's supposed to do, so he breaks it. The best thing you can do in Jeff's case is to try to think like Jeff. Put on your giant-alien-brain mask, get some coffee, clear your browser cache, reformat your hard drive, and try to forget everything you ever knew about your product. Then use it.

If you've decided to dogfood religiously, you'll want to follow some best practices to get the most mileage from your dogfood experience:

Plan a "dogfood release"
> The dogfood release is when you give your software to your colleagues within the company. It's a key milestone immediately after feature complete and before code complete. The dogfood release gives you a milestone where you show real progress. Also, soliciting your team's peers for kudos and feedback helps build the team's morale and ensure your product is on track.

Make it easy for others to send you bug reports
> Establishing a mailing list for dogfood bugs is a great way to monitor incoming defect volume. If you don't have a fast way for all of your dogfooders to enter bugs in your bug tracking system, you can easily create an online form in Google Docs that will organize and report on bugs. You can ask your test lead to write bugs based on these incoming email messages.

Continue to dogfood after you ship

Amazon and Google both maintain experimental frameworks that enable dogfooders to see specific features. These frameworks allow the software to run on production infrastructure but only be seen by internal users. It's a wise investment to build similar systems for your teams, because making your systems production ready can take significant time, and bugs take a while to emerge in dogfood. Having a framework that enables internal users to run on production systems allows you to collect feedback and complete production work in parallel.

Make dogfooding a core corporate value

It's pretty common to find that your colleagues don't dogfood. Or, if they do dogfood, they're too busy to file bugs. Shame on them! But whining won't get them to be better dogfooders. The best you can do is follow the previous suggestions and remind your colleagues to dogfood. If dogfooding isn't working, work to understand why and fix it. In the meantime, you can rely on trusted testers (more on them later).

How to Run a Bug Bash

A *bug bash* is an event where your team, or your whole company, takes a dedicated period of time—typically an hour—to find as many bugs in your dogfood product as possible. A good bug bash will almost certainly find a bunch of bugs that you'll want to fix. You'll want to do four things to encourage a good bug bash:

- Incentivize people to bug bash. Offer an award. T-shirts are shockingly effective.
- Make the bug bash a key milestone in your project plan. Schedule the bug bash so your entire extended team knows when it will happen and can get involved.
- Build bug bashes into your development and testing schedule.
- Say thank you for every bug. Remember, bad news is good news. Every bad bug is good news.

Triage Bugs Properly

I frequently ask product management candidates, "How do you triage bugs?" when I perform phone screens. I'm always amazed at how incomplete the answers are! I think bugs are as simple to triage as 1, 2, 3!

1. Grade bugs based on frequency, severity, and cost to fix.
2. Meet daily to review your new bugs with your dev lead and test lead.
3. Continually make it harder to accept new bugs as launch blockers. If you don't, you'll never hit zero bug bounce (ZBB), which means no launch blocking bugs are reintroduced. If you never hit ZBB, you'll never ship.

The first of these three steps is bug grading. Your goal is to figure out which bugs you should fix, and that's not as simple as fixing only the really bad ones, because some bugs are ugly and very easy to fix. So you need to look at three dimensions when you grade a bug:

Frequency

Frequency is your measure of how often the bug occurs. One time out of 10? Does it appear only when servers restart? Or maybe it happens every time a user logs in? The more frequently a bug occurs, the more important it is that you fix it.

Severity

You want to assess how damaging to the user experience the bug is. If the bug is a big security or privacy hole, it's a high-severity bug. If there's a spelling mistake, that's a low-severity bug, even if it is moderately embarrassing.

Cost to fix

That spelling mistake is really cheap to fix. A bug where you can't shard a user session across multiple servers, on the other hand, is going to be very expensive to fix, and you'll likely have to trade some features for that change.

After you and the team understand how you're going to grade the bugs, you enter step 2, in which you have a daily bug triage meeting to decide which bugs you will fix. The PM, the dev lead, and the test lead should get together and go through the bugs. The gotcha in this process is that it can take forever if the three of you try to figure out what is going on in each bug. And bug triage can be really boring. You want to try to move through your triage meeting as fast as possible. In triage, try to do the following:

Establish a general bug bar

For me, this bar starts at: "Would I be embarrassed if my high school buddies encountered this? And how many of them would encounter it? And would it do them any lasting damage if they hit the bug?" You, your dev lead, and your test lead may all have a different point of view on these dimensions, but you'll converge pretty quickly.

Move through the bugs from most severe to least severe

Your test team will provide an initial rating for bugs so that you get the worst bugs addressed quickly.

Allocate a specific amount of time for your triage

If you run out of time, continue the next day. This process will help you manage your energy.

Only talk about frequency, severity, and cost

One of the reasons you have a test lead in the triage meeting is so that he or she can comment on the cost of fixing a bug and also identify innocuous bugs that expose deeper, scarier flaws. Be vigilant and avoid deep dives into finding the root cause of every issue at this stage! If you find a bug that may be more severe than you thought, boost the severity rating and move on.

Spend less than one minute per bug

If you don't know what's going on with a bug, reassign to the reporter for clarification. If you need to investigate the bug further before you can triage, add that to a special list of "investigation bugs." The one-minute rule helps eliminate excessively detailed discussions. I've found that once you've conditioned the team to this pace, everyone wants to keep it going, because nobody likes bug triage.

After some time, you'll find that even though your bug count is going down nicely, new bugs keep popping up. This is the third step of triage: you have to keep moving the bug bar up, making it harder to declare that a bug is a launch blocker. As general guidance, this principle may seem counterintuitive. After all, you don't want to be embarrassed, right? The reality is that you're constantly writing new software, and that means you're introducing new bugs. If you want to hit ZBB, you have to stop adding bugs to the list of launch blockers. Progressively, and carefully, raise the bug bar as you get closer to launch.

Use Trusted Testers

Trusted testers are users under NDA (nondisclosure agreement) who use the dogfood version of your product before it ships. They are using different computers than your team, have different expectations, and are generally much less technical than you. As a result, their feedback is immensely valuable.

At Amazon, I had a group of trusted Customer Reviews writers who could give us great feedback. I gave them my direct email address—they frequently found production issues faster than my engineering team. They also didn't hesitate to email Jeff Bezos, and when they did, I got Jeff Mail. When you're a team lead and you get Jeff Mail, you drop everything and address it!

At Google, we had hundreds of businesses in the trusted tester program for Google Talk. We turned on the same experiments we used internally and asked them to send us bugs. They gave us great feedback and helped us pinpoint quality issues.

To make the trusted tester system work—which in the case of Talk meant we had ~15% active participation—I followed these best practices:

Have the businesses sign an NDA and provide the correct contact information
> The NDA for a trusted tester may need to be different than your hiring or business development NDAs because you want to protect your right to use any improvements that your customers suggest. Ask your lawyer for advice on what your NDA should include.

Create rough "getting started" documentation, including a list of known issues
> A Google Site is a nice way to aggregate these artifacts, because it's easy to share with arbitrary email accounts and can be updated very quickly and easily.

Create an email alias that delivers to the whole engineering team and from which you can email
> If you configure your email this way, replies will go to the whole team, not just to you. I'm a firm believer in bringing customers as close to the engineering team as possible. It helps make the software real, and that's motivating for an engineering team. It also may reduce your workload because your engineering team can help answer questions from their users.

Add these customers to the same dogfood experience that the engineering team uses

In some situations you may have a daily build that your engineering team uses, and you don't want your trusted testers on that. Daily builds are too unstable because they are not tested and change too quickly.

Survey your trusted testers

You can use Google Spreadsheets forms, or SurveyMonkey, to get a general impression of product quality. This survey is also a nice opportunity to get a sense of price sensitivity, since the users are actually experiencing the product.

Update your trusted testers on changes

With each email update you send, you'll find a little bounce in usage. Ideally, you can time your updates with software updates so you get some external test coverage.

Parting Thought: Use the Entire Product as a New User

It seems to me that it's always the little things that get you. If you're doing a good job dogfooding, you're not going to be embarrassed by the majority of your product. But some of the most complicated parts of your product form the out-of-the-box experience (meaning, "I just opened the box; what's inside?" not "Hmm, let's think outside the box now!"). Specific things to look for are how you create an account and populate that account with data. As a dogfooder, you probably performed those tasks only once, and that was four months ago!

Pinterest.com is a great example of how to create a brilliant out-of-the-box experience. It's incredibly easy to sign up—you use your Facebook account—and your landing page is great because Pinterest suggests people for you to follow and fills your page with lovely images that you care about.

Here's a tip to help ensure you experience what new users experience: when you hit feature complete and again when you hit code complete, make sure you delete all your data and accounts and start from scratch.

6

How to Measure Greatness

You can frequently assess the quality of a team by the quality of their metrics. Metrics are the lifeblood of a team lead because everything in your job is a negotiation, and metrics provide a rational foundation for discussion. If you don't back up your statements with metrics, you'll sound like Animal the Muppet. You also need metrics because you are constantly making judgment calls, and good data creates good (or at least defensible) judgment. Great leads live by their metrics because metrics point out problems, track progress, and celebrate success.

How to Collect the Right Metrics and Only the Right Metrics

There's a story, possibly apocryphal, that tells how Frito-Lay came up with one metric by which it could run its business. Frito-Lay stocks store shelves, taking up critical inventory space. Ideally, it will take up exactly the amount of space on a shelf that it needs—too much, and its products get returned. Too little, and it misses out on sales.

You can imagine multiple ways of figuring out how to create a metric for this business. You could sample the number of products on shelves every day and then forecast a trend, but that would be very time-consuming, especially if products are typically stocked every two weeks. You could measure store profitability and then look at stock levels, but that would deliver data that's confounded by store effectiveness and size.

Frito-Lay solved this problem by measuring "stales," the count of products that are returned at each restock event because the product is out of date. Frito-Lay wants the number of stales to equal precisely one. Taking a single bag of potato chips as a chargeback may seem a crime to you, but as a measurement cost it is very small. If the stales count is greater than one, the suppliers decrease the stock levels. If there are no stales, they increase the stock levels. It's a fabulously simple metric that the field can measure and to which the company can react.

From Frito-Lay's example, we can learn five key aspects of a great metric:

The metric is inexpensive to measure

Stales are a wonderful measure because the data already exists as chargebacks.

The metric can be measured reliably and repeatedly

Reliability and repeatability enable testing, which helps you ensure that your metric works. For example, if you were to swap out the chip stocker and you found that your stales count went up, you could investigate and determine that there was some different pattern of behavior. Perhaps the chips were stacked backward—certainly, displaying the nutrition information on Fritos is not going to help sales.

The metric is measured frequently, ideally in real time

One of the most remarkable systems I've seen implemented is Amazon's order tracking system. Amazon has enough orders and data that it creates a live, statistical process control model with orders. If your feature launches and damages order flow, you can rest assured that your pager will go off nearly instantly!

The metric enables your team to make smart changes

Like the Frito-Lay chip stocker who can react in real time to changing inventory conditions, your team needs to understand what to do when a metric changes. For example, even though Amazon's order measurement system is clearly brilliant, it's only a health metric. When an alarm goes off because orders are low or high relative to predictions, you know there is a problem, but you don't know where the problem is. Furthermore, it's great for a team to drive orders up, but the Amazon product is far too large for any team to measure their impact through the global ordering pipeline. But if your team is responsible for the shopping cart, and you measure the conversion ratio of users entering the checkout process to those who get a "Thanks for buying!" page, you will have a single number that reflects user experience and systems performance, and gives you a goal to target.

The metric focuses on the customer

Another reason I like the ordering conversion metric is that it's a number that reflects the customer experience. If your systems become too slow, or you add a lot of steps into the process for users, the metric will decline. But if you measured the 99.9% mean latency of the Oracle database at the backend and reported that metric, it might well have had no impact on the customer experience at all until it hit two or three seconds. Your goal should be to collect your data as close to the customer as possible. Metrics that are close to customers are meaningful and understandable.

Another aspect of focusing on the customer is measuring as late in the customer's experience as possible. For example, if you make downloadable iPhone software, which metric is more meaningful, downloads or application starts? I'd argue it's application starts, because downloads tell you only about marketing, whereas application starts tell you about user engagement and growth.

Your goal, therefore, is to identify the "stales" of your product. Before you go off creating a sophisticated algorithm by which to run your business, remember the fourth point, which says that you and your team need to be able to take action on a metric. Some businesses have a very hard time being run on a single number, and an attempt to do so renders the output meaningless; this was the case with many of the single-number "fitness functions" that Amazon tried to implement for its teams. While the Ordering team was able to generate a brilliant fitness function that they could live to, other teams had a far more difficult time and had to apply complex mathematical transformations to their data. Worse yet, they spent tons of engineering time coming up with the metrics! Down this path lies danger.

The Three Classes of Metrics You Should Collect

W. Edwards Deming once wrote "That which cannot be measured cannot be improved," and boy, was he right. What's more, if you work for a year on a brilliant product to improve some customer's life, but you can't measure its impact, how are you going to get promoted? And after you realize that you can't get promoted, how are you going to get a new job when you have no improvement to demonstrate?

If you're going to demonstrate improvement, you need a baseline. Therefore, you must establish metrics early and keep them updated throughout the development of your product. It's not hard to establish basic metrics. Consider, for example, your engineering team's ability to execute.

One measure of execution might be whether you can make your launch date. Your launch date is frequently a function of the number of bugs left to fix. Many bug tracking systems can generate find/fix ratios and bug counts as charts. Therefore, if you combine the find/fix ratio with a bug count, you can create a forecasted "zero bugs" date. For more on how to generate this metric and why it's important, see the section "Track Your Bugs and Build a Bug Burndown" in Chapter 4.

The zero bugs date is a great metric for your development process because it is nearly free with most bug tracking systems, it can be measured reliably and repeatedly, it can be reported in real time, and it provides direction to your team. In this latter case, if you are distracting your team with more of your "great ideas," your find/fix ratio will go up and push your ship date out. And since one of your goals is to minimize your ship date, you should quit it with the great ideas already!

Your metrics will probably change after you launch because you recently introduced a major new source of input: customers and customer usage. You'll use metrics based on customers and their actions to report to your investors or management, inform your product decisions, and guide your team. There are three critical classes of post-launch metrics: progress toward goals, business performance, and systems performance.

PROGRESS TOWARD GOALS

Goal metrics report your progress toward achieving an objective. One goal metric that is a staple at Google is the "seven-day active user count." It represents the number of unique users who used the product during the trailing seven days. This metric is much better than the typical "daily unique user count" you get out of cheap web metrics packages, because it measures current behavior and you can compare week-to-week performance easily. It's also much more reasonable than daily users, since you will rarely build a product that you expect people to use every day.

If you are building a product that you *do* expect customers to use every day, then the delta between one-day and seven-day active users is very meaningful. For example, when I worked on Google's plug-in for

Microsoft Outlook—Google Apps Sync for Microsoft Outlook™—we expected that people who were using Outlook would probably check their mail daily unless our software wasn't working well. Therefore, we paid close attention to the ratio of seven-day active users to one-day active users. If you have an infrequently used service, such as photo printing, you might care more about 30-day active users.

Other goals you might want to track include revenue, signups, downloads, or installs.

At this point you may be thinking, "I know all about goals. I know to make them S.M.A.R.T." What's S.M.A.R.T? Some rocket surgeon a while back came up with the notion that goals should be *specific*, *measurable*, *attainable*, *reasonable*, and *time-based*. This is a good, but not sufficiently specific, framework. I prefer the Great Delta Convention (described in Chapter 10). If you apply the Great Delta Convention to your goals, nobody will question them—they will almost be S.M.A.R.T. by definition (lacking only the "reasonable" part).

BUSINESS PERFORMANCE

Business performance metrics tell you where your problems are and how you can improve your user's experience. These metrics are frequently measured as ratios, such as conversion from when a user clicks the Buy button to when the checkout process is complete. Like goal metrics, it's critical to measure the right aspects of your business. For example, if you want to build a great social product, you don't need to measure friends—different segments of users have different numbers of friends. But you do want to measure user engagement so you can answer questions like "Are users spending time on the site?" and "Are they posting?" A relevant collection of metrics for these behaviors might be posts in seven days per seven-day-active-user and minutes spent on-site per seven-day active user.

Eric Ries isn't a big fan of these growth metrics in his book *The Lean Startup* (Crown Business). He calls them *vanity metrics* because you can puff up your chest, point to a chart that goes up and to the right, and say, "Look, we're awesome! We're growing!" even as your product is failing 90% of the incoming new users. It's a fair point. This is why you need to look at metrics like conversion and engagement, among others. Nearly all web analytics packages will provide conversion metrics out of the box, and they will also tell you which features are used, which buttons are clicked, and by which groups of users.

Another way to avoid "vanity" in your metrics is by measuring changes to your application. It's always best to test in real time, rather than longitudinally, because longitudinal analysis is fraught with confounding problems and you can easily say, "See, we're still going up!" Google Analytics provides A/B comparison tools that are incredibly powerful, but they're just one kind of many tools you can use. Most major websites have testing frameworks that they use to roll out features incrementally and ensure that a new feature or experience has the intended effect. If it's even remotely possible, try to build an experimentation framework in from the beginning (see Chapter 7's discussion of launching for other benefits of experiments).

SYSTEMS PERFORMANCE

Systems performance metrics measure the health of your product in real time. Metrics like these include 99.9% mean latency, total requests per second, simultaneous users, orders per second, and other time-based metrics. When these metrics go down substantially, something has gone wrong. A pager should go off.

If you're a very fancy person, you'll want to look at your metrics through the lens of *statistical process control* (SPC). W. Edwards Deming was one of the first to popularize SPC as a mathematical way of measuring how much a metric can decline before you should page your tech lead. He learned from Walter Shewart in the '20s. Deming assumes there is noise in your system, and within this noise there's an envelope of acceptable performance. This is considered *common cause* variation, or Type I error—noise, as it were.

Then there are spikes of badness over a smaller period of time. Deming calls this *special cause* variation, or Type II error. A bad push or a server falling out of a virtual IP (VIP) might cause such a spike.

You can ignore common cause error—your noise—if it falls within two standard errors of the mean. The standard error is defined as the standard deviation/$\sqrt{N}$ for the mean of your data. If a single data point falls outside of two standard errors of the mean, ring the pager.

Focus on the Goal, Not the Minutiae

It is generally true that any metric can be gamed. To continue with our previous launch date example, we could categorize more bugs as not launch blockers, or we could simply stop testing (which seems like a win-win on its face!). In reality, you and your team are unlikely to game the system because the metric is only an indicator—not the boss—so don't worry if your core metrics can be gamed. When the metric becomes the boss and you spend days and weeks trying to justify the number, it's time to change the metric. Or go work somewhere else.

7

How to Have a Great Launch

CONGRATULATIONS! YOU HAVE (ALMOST) no more bugs to fix, you've built a product that your trusted testers love, and your team is proud of what they built. You have the system instrumented so you'll know when you're doing well. You even have a rough cut of a blog post from way back when you first defined the product.

It's time to launch, and launching is more complicated than uploading files to a server. There are several major launch steps you can follow to ensure a quality launch:

1. Just say no.
2. Start a war room.
3. Instill a sense of urgency in the team.
4. Complete the launch checklist.
5. Write the blog post.
6. Roll the software out.
7. Verify the software yourself.
8. Respond to the positive and negative effects of your launch.

Just Say No

When you're driving to launch, you must say no as often as possible to features, to bugs, and to changes in the user experience. If you don't say no, you'll never finish your software and you'll never ship. There's an industry aphorism that goes, "You launch the software you have, not the software you want." This aphorism is sticky within the software industry because it's true—sometimes you just have to ship your product, even when it's not perfect, because shipping something good is better than not shipping something perfect. Most of us can agree that this statement is true, but it's hard to enforce because the definition of "good" is arbitrary.

To remove some of the arbitrariness from this stage of the project, I check to ensure that the team feels proud. Your team must be proud of the software they build, and the bugs you have in the product shouldn't embarrass you. Beyond those caveats, you have to be willing to live with the decisions that you made months and weeks ago. One way to enable the team to say no is to create a list of things to change "immediately post-launch" (IPL). By enabling the team to understand that some changes shouldn't block the launch but are the first things to change after you ship, you'll help the team feel better about the product because they know their concerns will be addressed soon.

Another major reason you should say no to late-breaking changes is that almost any change to your code—aptly termed *code motion*—risks introducing new bugs or reintroducing old bugs. Reopening old bugs or having functionality that used to work fail is considered a *regression*. Teams frequently cope with avoiding regressions and continuing to move forward by creating a *release branch*. The release branch is a version of your software that you intend to ship, and you add code to this branch only if that code fixes critical problems. Development of new features can continue on a *development branch*. This process works well but adds overhead, because the engineering team must make changes to both the release branch and the development branch. While the engineering effort to maintain these branches is not double, it is a significant additional cost, so defer to your development lead when it comes to defining your branches.

I push very hard to maintain a release branch, for the simple reason that it gives my teams a way to cope with crisis. Because a release branch isn't supposed to change after release, if you discover a major failure, such as a security, privacy, or major performance problem, you can apply that single "hotfix" to the release branch. The tests you need to perform on the release branch are therefore small and quick, because the change is isolated and nothing else has changed. Since your change and your tests were completed quickly, you can release the hotfix very soon after you discover the problem.

Run a War Room

As you get close to launch, your meetings must change. Your weekly meetings are now unnecessary because everyone is aligned with the mission and moving quickly. At this point, you can rely on standup meetings and relax the rule that participants must take all issues offline. Moving quickly is critical if you're going to make the launch, and some issues are best resolved quickly even if resolving them means that half the team is stand-ing around idly. Standup meetings help you make rapid decisions and help communicate a sense of urgency to the team.

Because these standups are a bit more involved, they become more like a war room, in which people huddle together in a closet to work out emerging issues. The reality of your software release is that systems are so complicated and prone to fussy little failures that sometimes a war room is a great way to force coordination and eliminate downtime between hand-offs. If the people who need to hand off are sitting next to each other, the hand-off time is effectively zero.

Instill a Sense of Urgency

One could argue that you've failed to manage your project well if you're in the late stages of a project and there is a heightened sense of urgency. It does seem to follow that a well-organized and planned project should come in right on time. Real software projects don't follow theory, though, and all projects seem to expand to fit the time allotted and end in a sprint. I've never seen it work otherwise, so embrace it, and remember that the time to maintain your cool is when others are losing theirs!

I believe that a single sprint to the finish is not bad. A sprint that lasts less than a month is tolerable by most teams and families, particularly since you'll give the team time to rest on the other side. A death march is when the sprint starts long before the release and continues after it. Death marches are evil. They destroy teams, they create bad software, and they're no fun. Do not ask your team to sprint for more than a month, or maybe two at the outside. If your date is unrealistic and you need to push it, it's your job to grit your teeth and take the message upstairs, even though you know you are coming back down the stairs with a s#!@ sandwich (see Chapter 12). Send the message now, before your team starts to sprint.

If you know this sprint is the real deal, the best thing you can do during your final sprint is ensure that your dependencies and supporting teams share your sense of urgency. Less experienced engineers are gener-ally hesitant to escalate to other teams or ask for help. They are afraid of having people find out what they don't know. This reticence makes psycho-logical sense, because admitting you don't know what to do requires some maturity; generally, the people who know the most are the first to admit they don't know how to fix a problem. Make sure your development lead is paying attention to your less experienced engineers.

One way of instilling a sense of urgency in your dependencies is by calling them on the phone and brokering discussions between your team and their team. The conversation is likely to be a negotiation, so agree on goals first, and then work to come up with a creative solution (see Chapter 11 for tips on how to negotiate). Also remember that your job is not to solve the problem, but rather to facilitate the development of a solution to the problem. When you do get people on the phone together, make sure they're speaking the same language and communicate your own sense of urgency to your dependencies.

Complete the Launch Checklist

A great launch needs a launch checklist. The goal of the checklist is to ensure that all of the moving pieces of your software launch are aligned and scripted. The launch checklist also facilitates communication across the different functions of your team. Checklists are incredibly powerful when used properly; every single commercial pilot goes through a checklist on every single commercial airplane flight—that's how powerful and important checklists are.

Each of your leads, from design to test, will have items in the checklist. There's no perfect checklist for every project (each plane has its own, after all) and each subteam—such as legal, test, or marketing—may have its own subchecklists. But do your best and add items you know you need to track. A simple example checklist is shown in Figure 7-1 and is available for download at *http://www.shippinggreatness.com*.

PM Launch Checklist

Launch Date: 08/25/11 starting 2200 PST   Project Site: http://sites.google.com/a/domain.com/helloworld

Area	Item	Owner	Status	Due	Reference
Engineering					
	Bug Bash	Chris, PM	Done	7/15/2011	http://bugzilla/123
	Metrics Dashboard	Chris, PM	Done	8/1/2011	http://www/dash
	Capacity Plan, capacity	Sally, eng	In Progress	8/1/2011	
	Zero Bug Bounce	Larry, test	Open	8/10/2011	
	Cut release branch	Sally, eng	Done	8/15/2011	build 0731
	Security Review	Sally, eng	Done	8/1/2011	
Operations					
	Notify all dependent services	Chris, PM	Open	8/10/2011	
	On Call rotation	Sally, eng	Done	8/20/2011	http://www/oncall
	Trademark Review	Ed, Legal	Open	8/1/2011	
	Patent review	Ed, Legal	In Progress	8/1/2011	
	Privacy review	Ed, Legal	Open	8/1/2011	
	Blog post	Martin, PR	In Progress	8/15/2011	
Day of launch					
	Push to Prod	Sally, Eng	Open	8/25/2011	
	Post-push verification	Larry, Test	Open	8/25/2011	
	Experiment to 1%	Sally, Eng	Open	8/25/2011	
	Experiment to 10%	Sally, Eng	Open	8/25/2011	
	Experiment to 100%	Sally, Eng	Open	8/25/2011	
	Push blogpost	Chris, PM	Open	8/25/2011	

Figure 7-1. Launch checklist

Write the Blog Post

If you've followed the detailed product development process, you've already written your blog post—or at least written the press release, which has the same objective. Your goal for the blog post is to state your mission, the customer to whom you're speaking, and what problem you are solving. This is your "lede" in the classic journalism sense. For example, here is a great example from the beginning of the Google+ launch blog post:

> Among the most basic of human needs is the need to connect with others. With a smile, a laugh, a whisper or a cheer, we connect with others every single day.
>
> Today, the connections between people increasingly happen online. Yet the subtlety and substance of real-world interactions are lost in the rigidness of our online tools.
>
> In this basic, human way, online sharing is awkward. Even broken. And we aim to fix it.

Google targets a clear group of people: those who want to share online. It has identified a problem: online sharing is "rigid" and "awkward." And in the subsequent paragraphs, it drills into the four unique ways in which it will solve this awkwardness. If Google can do this with the launch of a product that was not all that different from one that already existed, imagine what you can do!

Your goal is to build the same quality blog post. Leverage your draft press release, veer away from the details while still using specific examples, and work with marketing to make it great. This is your chance to add sizzle, but do it in keeping with your corporate tone.

The blog post is your script for your demo. Plan to include a one-and-a-half to three-minute video following the post, so that users who don't have access to your product or the patience to try it can still experience the great software you built.

Roll the Software Out

The best way to roll out a feature is through an experimental framework. Experiments are great because both the old code and the new code live on your production servers at the same time, which enables you to flip back and forth between version 1 and version 2 extremely quickly and without having to restart servers. The investment to build an experimental framework almost always pays off longer term.

If you've watched major sites like Google and Amazon change, you may have noticed that some users get a different experience than others, because both are using experiments to deploy and test features. Amazon calls these releases Weblabs, because they measure how the new software impacts users, compared to the group of users who don't have the new software. Yes, some of your users will have a different experience than the majority of your users, but that's OK. It turns out that users don't mind. And if they do mind, roll back and thank your lucky stars you planned to roll back!

Google has free systems in Google Analytics you can use to build your own Weblab-like releases. I've used them and they're great. One team I led ran a series of experiments through Google Analytics and we increased conversion by 65%—Google Analytics provided us with that data.

There can be challenges to implementing this experimental approach, though. When your service has underlying data model changes, you may be unable to roll back, or you may have disjointed data sets. These are tricky problems, and it's always best if you can avoid them entirely by making your data models backward compatible. Easier said than done, I know, but the benefit of being able to roll back without losing user data is a big win.

No matter how hard you try, it's very challenging to get a launch right the first time. Building in a mechanism that enables you to ensure that you got everything connected and configured before millions of users see your product is incredibly valuable.

A word on timing: don't launch on Friday or right before the holidays. Not only do you miss the press cycle, but also the last thing you want to do is roll out a bunch of software and then desperately page people all weekend. I once foolishly agreed to roll out some software on December 18 to take advantage of holiday PC buyers, only to find that my pager went off when our service started to fail and I had to call engineers around the country at dinnertime on Christmas Eve. No joke.

Verify the Software Yourself

After you've pushed all your services to production, you want to verify the push in two ways. First, your test lead should orchestrate a verification pass, also known as a *build verification test* (BVT), which is typically run after doing a build of your software. By doing this, your test lead ensures that the right version of software was pushed to your production servers and that all the configuration was also pushed and set up correctly. It's easy to miss little details, even if they're simple, like making sure *http://domain.com* can handle traffic, not just *http://www.domain.com*!

Second, you need to personally go through the experience as a new user and ensure that all the major functions are working. Things that typically fail are signup processes, any form of data upload (like images), searching, and form submissions. These items tend to fail because they rely on subsystems and are sometimes configured to point to the wrong servers. These types of failures happen all the time. Your team should wait to roll out to a larger percentage of users until you, your test lead, and your development lead all sign off. This may seem like a lot of process, but it's really just three people connected on IM, so it's not bad.

Respond to the Positive and Negative Effects of Your Launch

If you've signed off on your verification pass, then congratulations—you've done a great job and your software has launched! But there are a few things remaining before you can consider your great software to have shipped. You need to deal with any crises that emerge, announce the product to the world, and celebrate with your team. Here are the five post-launch tasks you'll need to complete:

1. Handle any rollbacks.
2. Cope with production crises.
3. Demo the product.
4. Handle the press.
5. Celebrate your launch.

IN THE CASE OF PROBLEMS, ROLL THE SOFTWARE BACK

Successful rollback is not failure. This bears repeating: *successful rollback is not failure*. A rollback is when you revert your software to its prelaunch state. Rollbacks are more common than you might think. I've seen releases take five attempts or more at both Amazon and Google. Large software systems have so many complicated interfaces and dependencies that it's nearly impossible to test and validate every possible permutation before you launch. If you roll back and there was no significant customer damage, you haven't been successful, but you haven't failed yet. Therefore, in the end, the best defense is a well-planned retreat.

There are times when you can't roll back or when rollbacks are so expensive that doing so isn't justifiable. In situations where you can't roll back, your best bet is to make sure that you have the team capacity to keep moving forward very quickly for a couple of days, because it may take you that long to find and fix your problems—and as you're fixing them, customers are having a bad day. On the other hand, if rollback is possible, you can turn off the changes, fix things at a leisurely pace, and try again.

HANDLE ANY PRODUCTION CRISES

Sometimes the world explodes. Maybe you got slashdotted. Or maybe there was a security hole, privacy violation, or pricing mishap. Or maybe an intern redirected the production website to his or her desktop instead of the datacenter (true story!). In cases like these, there's a good script you can follow. And like all good reactive measures, it's inspired by the Boy Scouts: you start by being prepared.

Part of being prepared means having an on-call rotation and pagers. I still haven't seen cell phones work as reliably as pagers, but I also haven't found a reliable way of forcing engineers outside of Amazon to carry pagers. Have the cell phone numbers of every engineer in your team on your phone or in your pocket.

A well-prepared product has software switches that can easily turn off or rate-limit your service. Remember to launch experimentally or with flags to disable your feature if at all possible. Remember, successful rollback is not failure!

You can prepare for disaster well ahead of time by having great design review meetings. In your reviews, you want to ensure that the engineering team designs for failure. You can do this by building logic that limits requests to overloaded servers. You'll want this backoff to escalate exponentially, and always have a random modifier in the amount you back off so that the act of backing off doesn't create further mayhem. The random modifier is no joke—I've seen the backoff mechanism take down more systems than the original problem did. Make sure that the backoff mechanism exists before you ship.

You'll be better prepared if you know how to get in touch with a server genius even if you don't have one on your team. Even better, maintain, publish, and know your emergency contacts. Create an internal wiki with your PR, legal, and cross-functional team contacts. There's little more frustrating than trying to figure out whom in PR you need to talk to when your feature is suddenly behaving badly to a specific ethnic group for no apparent reason. And yes, this happened to me.

Establishing good communication paths in advance works the other way too: build a *<service>-escalation@yourcompany.com* alias so the right people can get involved. This alias should probably include PR, customer support, you, your engineering and production leads, and essential cross-functional owners. Also subscribe your team alias to this list, because escalations are a great teaching device!

If there's an ongoing risk (e.g., a launch), make sure all relevant parties know that there could be a problem. You must be willing to bother people to ask for help, but if the crisis is large you probably won't have a hard time admitting that your pants are on fire.

The final thing you need to do to be prepared is print out the next two sections, tape them to your wall, and work through them like a playbook for when s#!@ hits the fan.

Crisis playbook: Minutes 0–5

❏ **Don't panic.**
This is harder than it looks. If your boss is on the phone, the odds are good that he or she is panicking. It doesn't seem to matter how much the bosses are paid or how experienced they are. Get them off the phone as fast as possible so you can go back to not panicking.

❏ **Verify that there's an emergency and assess the extent of the damage.**
You want to assess the percentage of your user base that's affected and how severely. If you're lucky, it's not that big of a deal. Since you're reading this book, and you work in software, it's unlikely that you're lucky, so read on.

❏ **Make sure it's not just you.**
Sometimes your computer or your account can end up in a strange state. The last thing you want to do is run around with your pants on fire when the only problem was that you cleared your cookies. You also want to make sure the problem is not specific to internal users within your company or a "dogfood" artifact. In addition to verifying with external accounts, you probably want to check for external customer reports in discussion forums, Twitter, eHarmony—whatever you use. You're looking for a corroborating customer.

If the problem is a big deal, treat it like it's a big deal. Don't work too hard to convince yourself it's not a big deal and that not that many customers are affected. Convincing yourself that it's all going to be fine when really the situation is a disaster is not going to help. You can understand that you're going to get fired and still not panic. Sure, that's counterintuitive, but if you haven't been there, you will be.

❏ **Set up a conference call.**

If you are running the concall, *do not try to solve the problem*. I empha-sized this advice on purpose. It is very hard not to solve the problem when you know a lot about your systems and care passionately about your customers. However, your job on the concall is to facilitate the conversation, not solve the problem. If you try to solve the problem, you'll only add confusion. I know this sounds counterintuitive, but many managers have learned this. If you want to try to learn it your-self, go ahead...

❏ **Open a bug.**

You'll use this bug to record changes that you make to your systems. When engineers get log snippets, they can add them to the bug. People can add themselves to the bug if they want to listen in on the technical conversation. This bug will be very useful when you write the post-mortem because it will have timestamps and good documentation on what you did right and what you did wrong.

❏ **Notify your escalation alias.**

Send email to the email list you set up in advance and engage the first person on the escalation path, whether that's PR, engineering, or someone at the network operations center. Make sure you get a positive acknowledgment, either by the phone, pager, or email. It's not enough to leave a voicemail.

Crisis playbook: Minutes 5–30

❏ **Ask, "Can we roll it back?"**

The best way to fix any substantial crisis is to undo the change that caused it. "Rolling forward" requires more code, more testing, and therefore more time. It's best to avoid writing code under extreme pressure, so try to roll back first.

❏ **Postpone any planned PR.**

Frequently, but not always, you'll encounter a problem when you launch. If you have marketing, PR, or other plans that would draw additional traffic to your now-defunct product, make sure you put those operations on hold.

❏ **Let your dependent services know you are having a problem.**

Don't assume that you're the only one having a problem—make sure that your outage isn't hurting someone else. If you're hurting others, tell them so that they can work through the checklist themselves. They might have marketing plans too! Similarly, you want to make sure that you aren't being hurt by some other service. Occasionally, a major shared subsystem, like your backend storage, will go down and wreak havoc. In situations like these, the good news is that there's nothing you can do. The bad news is that there's nothing you can do, so add yourself to their bug (assuming they are following our process!) and watch it closely.

❏ **Notify your community.**

If you have a community forum or any way you typically communicate with your customers, you may want to let your customers know that "There seems to be a problem with X. We're actively investigating and will have more information/solution by time T." Google's Apps Status dashboard (*http://www.google.com/appsstatus*) is a great example of how to do this well. Use your PR/customer support team to help draft this note, so that you don't reveal something sensitive or overly frightening. It is, however, OK to admit that you had a problem. Customers appreciate honesty.

❏ **Keep your bug updated.**

Remember, people from other teams are looking for updates, and engineers are watching the bug to get additional background information. It's hard to tell when a small update will have substantial impact on your ability to make progress; be generous with your updates to the bug.

❏ **Find and introduce experts to consult with the team.**

Some problems are difficult to solve. Your team will probably solve any issue with enough time, but if your problem is directly impacting customers on an ongoing basis, you may not be willing to wait for your team to figure out the problem. Consider bringing in an expert from another team to help. You'll want to be careful as you do this, since you don't want to undermine or randomize your engineering team, but a very experienced engineer will generally know how to work well with your beleaguered team.

❏ **Inform your management.**

At this point your team knows what's going on, since you sent a note to your escalation alias. But your bosses don't know, and they need to know because they don't want *their* bosses to send a nastygram for which they are unprepared. So put your manager's email on the To: line, fill out the following MadLib, and hit Send.

> Team,
>
> We are actively working on a problem with _____. This means
> noun
>
> _____.
> 2 sentences describing
the user pain
>
> We estimate that _____ have been affected since _____.
> number of users   event start
> We estimate the impact is _____.
> how much data or revenue
is lost, etc.
>
> _____ and _____ are the solution owners. Their next steps
> engineer   concall lead
> are _____.
> verbs
>
> We estimate we'll have a fix at _____. Barring that, we'll have an
> time
> update in _____.
> time less than
2 hours
>
> This is the tracking bug: _____. Please watch the bug for more
> bug number
> information. In addition, we're running a concall that you can join at
>
> _____
> IRC or concall number
>
> _____,
> term of endearment
>
> _____
> your formal title and name

Crisis playbook: Minutes 31–N

Sometimes a crisis is going to last longer than a few hours. This is when you turn to your second in command and repeat what my first boss at Amazon told me: "This is going to suck for a while, but then it's going to be OK." After you've made this proud, bold, managerial statement, you need to move into long-term mode and start fixing things again. At this point, there are no quick and easy checklists. Rather, there are things you must do every day, including:

- Send status updates regularly and when you said you will. If people are asking for updates, you're not sending them often enough. Delivering status reports on time will help reassure your bosses that the problem is being solved well.
- Don't keep customers hanging. Set expectations about the problem and keep them informed. Try to underpromise and overproduce, because you get relatively few chances to make good with customers.
- Keep working the issue. People naturally get tired of working on just one thing, particularly when it's a firefighting project. Without your sense of urgency, your team could lose focus.
- Make sure that the people who are working on it have what they need—get them food, servers, support from other teams, etc.
- Set up a shift so that you don't have one developer working 24 hours. During one crisis at Amazon, I had an engineer say to me, "It's 3 a.m. and I don't think I can write any bug-free code right now." I appreciate that kind of honesty.
- Start building workarounds and contingency plans. Specifically, find ways to replace the failing systems with something else temporarily. For example, at Google we hit a capacity problem with our download servers at one point. We fixed this problem temporarily by shunting download traffic to Akamai's content delivery network.

Crisis playbook: Coping with the aftermath and writing a postmortem

Pat yourself on the back—you've fixed the problem, and the bosses are probably not going to fire you until tomorrow morning when they start reading their email. So get out your thumb drive, start copying your music, and follow the next steps:

1. Monitor your fix. Be double-sure that you fixed the problem; it's never good to be in a place where your team's judgment is questioned and you say, "We're 100% sure we fixed the problem," only to find out that you should have said "99% sure." Just like when you verify software yourself before you launch it, verify the fixes personally.
2. Prepare a blog post if you or your PR team thinks outward communication is warranted.

3. Build the action items into your team roadmap and update your business's stakeholders with their progress.
4. Write a postmortem.

A *postmortem* is a data-based apology for your management. A good postmortem is pretty easy to write, because you can structure it like you structured your third grade papers: What, Who, When, Why, and How. These questions are in this order to make it easier for your execs to get the answers they want in the order in which they tend to ask questions. Your bosses are likely to ask these questions as follows:

What happened?
   To answer this question, lay out the condensed timetable that describes when the issue first occurred, when it was discovered, when your team engaged, when it was fixed, and any other relevant milestones.

Whom did this affect?
   You want to be as specific as possible when talking about your customers. You want to say how many of them were affected, which subset of customers was affected, and anything else you know about them that might be relevant.

When did it start; when did it end?
   You should provide a basic timeline for the crisis.

Why did this happen?
   The "Why" section is where you explain the root cause. If you don't have a root cause, keep asking "why?" until you do (see Chapter 10's discussion of fishbone diagrams for some tips on this). You don't necessarily need to build out the discussion, as I do in the upcoming sidebar, but it may help explain why you reached the conclusions in the postmortem.

How will you prevent this type of problem in the future?
   If you have one great fix, that's fantastic (albeit unlikely). But if you're writing a postmortem, you probably have many things your team could do differently, so call them all out. To make sure that one or more of these changes happen, ensure that a single individual takes ownership for the change.

A hypothetical postmortem, also known as a "Cause Of Error" (COE) report, appears in the sidebar "Sample COE Report."

Sample COE Report

COE #1 – SQL injection hack causes humiliation.
03/07/12 — DRAFT — Chris Vander Mey (cvandermey@)

TRACKING BUG:
http://bugzilla/b=1234

WHAT was the problem?
The Ads Optimizations team released an update to the frontend of our optimizer that didn't correctly clean search statements. In parallel, the Database Operations team had updated our databases and rewritten some stored procedures that didn't correctly protect against SQL injection either. An intern discovered this problem while working on a starter project.

WHO did this impact?
Customers who were broken by this exposure experienced no customer-facing change. We performed an analysis of all SQL transaction logs and did not find any nonconforming INSERT/UPDATE/DELETE/SELECT…INTO statements, so we believe there was no customer-facing exploit. There were no customer reports of problems related to the outage.

The potential exposure, given where this break was featured, was ~10% of our user base, and required that the user have an account, which mitigated impact.

WHEN did this occur?

Issue started:	5/1/08	14:00
Issue discovered:	5/5/08	15:00
Rolled back to last-known-good server:	5/5/08	16:43
Issue resolved by pushing a new frontend:	5/6/08	16:00

Sample COE Report (continued)

WHY did this happen?

We don't have unit tests for SQL injection.
Why? We can't run builds against SQL servers effectively.
- Why? We aren't mocking the SQL servers.
  - Why? **We had a hole in our essential test matrix.**

We didn't coordinate with DB Ops.
Why? DB Ops is intentionally separate from our frontend teams, to add autonomy.
- Why? Things got really slow when we had teams discussing.
  - Why? Everyone had different opinions and we couldn't make decisions.
    - Why? **There was no clear ownership and accountability around who is responsible for query security.**

HOW will we avoid this problem in the future?
cvandermey@: Write unit tests to ensure that SQL injection fails.
harry_the_db_lead@: Write predeployment checklist and get signoff from product leads on each team that relies on DB Ops. Run aforementioned tests against all DB release candidates.
All TLs: Reinforce importance of code reviews. Charlie_tl@, in particular, write a checklist for things to look for in code reviews.

DEMO YOUR PRODUCT

We're back to the fun stuff, where your launch is going smoothly and now you need to show it off with a demo. Your demo should be straightforward; the goal of the demo is to tell the story from the blog post and reinforce your message at every step. It must be brief, probably less than 10 minutes, in order to hold the audience's attention. Your video on the blog post can't be a 10-minute video, however; videos need to be 90 seconds or less to hold someone's attention.

In the same way you wrote your blog post, the demo must be on-message. Start your demo with the problem statement and your message. Continually stating your message may feel repetitive, but it works. Start your demo by explaining why people should care about it.

Next, use your demo to tell a customer story. Great presentations use stories to draw listeners in and make the ideas real (more in Chapter 10 on presentations). Start your demo with a customer story and use that story to walk through your demo. Statements like "Imagine if..." and "People have a problem..." will help you tell the story and hook the audience. As you go through your demo, don't worry about the details of what you are trying to show. If some small thing goes wrong, skip over it and use the distraction as an opportunity to reiterate your core message.

While you can certainly skip over small defects in your presentation, the best cure for problems is to not have them. The best demos take weeks of preparation. Steve Jobs was notorious for demanding in-depth rehearsals, and it shows in the output of Apple's keynotes. In addition, Apple always thinks about how it can reduce the points of failure in a demo.

Microsoft product managers think the same way and routinely have three laptops: their personal laptop, their demo laptop, and their backup demo laptop. This approach gives them multiple backup strategies and ensures a stable demo environment. Personally, when I need to show something online, I bring hotspots from two different wireless providers and always try to use a wired connection when I can.

Despite all these warnings, if you're doing a demo at a live event, no amount of backup is sufficient. You must have screenshots or video for every part of your demo, because you can never fully predict what will go wrong. The launch of GoogleTV was riddled with technical problems and was painful to watch. In contrast, Apple's launch of the iPad 2 had similar problems but cut away to screenshots while the team forcibly disabled all WiFi access for attendees to the event, thereby remedying the problem. You want to be as prepared as Apple was, not as prepared as Google was.

HANDLE PRESS AND CUSTOMERS

If you have the good fortune to be contacted by the press or bloggers (it's good to remember that bloggers prefer to be thought of as press), you can make the most of it by engaging deeply. Take the calls and do demos. Respond quickly because most of the writers are on a deadline. If a writer posts something that is factually incorrect, reach out with a courteous correction—reporters may publish a correction. However, by the time the content is published it's usually too late for the reporter to do anything about it.

It is not too late, however, to respond online. First, you can respond directly to articles that are published online through their existing comment systems. Be clear and factual, and attribute the comments directly to you so that you're transparent and others can reach out to you. In the past I've published my email address directly in these forums in order to respond to contentious issues, and I've rarely been disappointed by the reaction I've encountered.

Second, you can respond to comments that others make, particularly if you have a user group. One of the most valuable ways you can spend your time immediately after launch is handling support requests and conversing with users in groups online. Users will tell you what you've done wrong, what's not working (even if you think it is), and what you need to add. If you listen closely in the weeks immediately after you launch, you'll be able to adjust your roadmap based on real customer input, and that will lead you to a very successful second version of your product.

CELEBRATE YOUR LAUNCH!

Every significant product release is enabled by many small (or sometimes large) sacrifices, and it's critical that you acknowledge what your team gave. Post-launch high-fives of any kind are basically free and can help readjust your team's point of view. For example, after working on Google's "Google Apps Sync for Microsoft Outlook" project for two years, I put together some basic metrics on early adoption that I shared with the team. I was able to use those metrics to pat the team on the back and get them some exposure to the senior leadership, and in turn the team was able to use those numbers to make their promotion cases. Your team will like you more if you get them promoted.

With teams at Amazon I brought in champagne for each launch, and the team signed the bottle. We put each bottle on a shelf in the office, creating a memento that stood as a reminder for the office of how great it is to ship.

Ideally, you want to celebrate your launch as close as possible to the time you launch. Keeping the timing of the celebration close to the sacrifices helps tie rewards and thanks to the actual sacrifices and accomplishments. But please, don't have a party during the launch. This guidance may be counterintuitive, but I once saw a program manager at Amazon have a launch party with food, beer, and paper plates (high-end for Amazon!) as his product rolled out. I asked him, "How's it going?" and he said, "Good!" thinking I meant the party. I was actually asking about the launch.

I went down the hall and most of his engineering team was sitting in their cubes, watching server health. It's really demoralizing when your team members can't go to their own party. The other dimension of this is that you don't want to celebrate too early. Frequently, you'll need to roll back a launch or sprint for another couple of days to fix emergent production problems. Ideally, you want your team to get past that panic and then celebrate and thank them for their effort.

Individual accolades are critical as well, but it can be both dangerous and helpful to compliment specific members of the team very publicly. Before you do so, have a good reason for why you want to make a public statement. Because everything is a teaching opportunity, I sometimes use stellar successes as a way of pointing out to the team what greatness looks like, so they know what to shoot for.

Be careful with public accolades. A Google VP once defended a generous perk he gave his team by saying, "They've worked really hard and I wanted to do something nice for them." This was broadly interpreted by Googlers-at-large as, "My team works harder than you, blah blah blah." Foot, meet bullet. He would have been much better served to associate that perk with a specific accomplishment. Also, when a single person does something truly unique and is OK with being singled out, go for it. But if there's any question, take that person to lunch and thank him or her one-on-one. You don't want to embarrass your teammates.

Part Two

The Shipping Greatness Skills

You are probably already pretty good at shipping software. But I'll wager you can be better. You can always be more efficient, for example. You could probably communicate more clearly. You could be less stressed out. You could have a bigger engineering team, more leverage with your senior management, or a better understanding of systems design. Or maybe none of these things applies to you and you can skip Part II entirely and send me your résumé.

If you are like most of us, you struggled to build one or more of these skills as you tried to ship software. Shipping software is unlike most other kinds of jobs because it requires precision technical communication, deep knowledge across a host of disciplines, and fortitude. The skills I emphasize in these chapters are tried-and-true methods for increasing your effectiveness and happiness—which in turn will help you ship.

Because you can't ship without a team, Chapter 8 covers how to hire or build a team, how to acquire a business when that is an option, how to work with offshore resources when you can't build a team locally, and how to join a team when there's one in place.

Chapter 9 describes what you need to know to be sufficiently technical so that you can work effectively with the engineers you hired in Chapter 8. This chapter is not a computer science course; rather, it's a fast-paced overview of the kinds of systems-oriented knowledge you need to be able to understand in order to guide your engineering team to the right decisions. If you hold a master's degree in computer science from Carnegie Mellon, please don't write me letters, just remember that I've seen very smart graduates with master's degrees in computer science create unfortunate architectures, which is why I added this section.

Because I can't teach you how to come up with great ideas that your team can build, Chapter 10 focuses on explaining how to communicate your already great ideas in the most efficient way possible. This chapter describes how to write an ideal email message, how to build a great presentation that accomplishes your goals, and how to run the five types of meetings successfully.

Of course, as you communicate your product and progress to others, they are going to provide feedback. Some of that feedback will be good, and some of it will be mind-bogglingly inane. Chapter 11 provides some techniques for dealing with the bad advice. It also discusses what feedback you should take, and how to make the right decisions as a team.

If you know how to build a good team, understand your technology, and can communicate well, you are in a great position to be successful. However, every day you're going to deal with some shipping-specific challenges, like feature requests and senior-management BS. Handling these challenges gracefully will reduce your cortisol levels and prolong your life. Chapter 12 discusses how to be great in the day-to-day of shipping.

If you've made it this far, you've learned that shipping is great and you're ready to do it again. Chapter 13 explains how to start the process all over again.

If you grow strong in these skills, you'll be one of the most capable team leads in the universe. I fully believe this. I also believe that the challenge is not understanding these skills, but actually acting on them in a consistent way. Good luck!

8

How to Build a Shipping-Ready Team

AFTER YOU DEFINE A great product idea and generate strong organization support, you need to pull together a team that can build and ship that product. Building the right team is the most important thing you can do, after choosing the right user problem to solve. A brilliant team can also end up being a durable competitive advantage. Most important, a great team helps eliminate problems in all the remaining steps of your software development.

Think about it: if you have a terrible designer, you'll end up reworking the same feature three times as you get randomized by user feedback. Bad systems design from a second-rate development lead will cause bizarre outages that will negatively impact users and cause your developers to stay up late, cursing each other and their pagers. And a bad product manager—they're the worst—will constantly randomize your team with a poorly thought-out set of bad ideas.

On the other hand, a great team is fun, makes you feel like you can accomplish anything, and will lead to lifetime friendships and profit. You must have a great team, and you can play an essential role in team building regardless of your explicit title. Here's how to do it.

How to Start a Team

To start a team effectively, you must find engineering, product, and design leads with whom you can work well. When you find these individuals, treasure them. Write them poems, buy them candy, and offer to wash their cars. You are only as effective as your engineering team, so finding a leader who can run a well-oiled engineering machine will radically offload work from you and substantially accelerate your other efforts. Throughout the industry, you'll find that the same people work together across businesses and projects for precisely this reason.

It is impossible to care too much about your team, its quality, and the happiness of your team members. Read Beverly Kaye and Sharon Jordan-Evans's book *Love 'Em or Lose 'Em* (Berrett-Koehler) and practice what it preaches, even if you're not a people manager. It talks about how to retain your best people and get the most out of them. Leads can have a substantial impact on the careers and happiness of their teammates by doing things like directing the right projects, problems, or recognition to people who need it. *Love 'Em or Lose 'Em* will give you great ideas for actions you can take and techniques for figuring out what actions will work.

Frequently, the job of a team lead is too much work for a single person to accomplish. The job is nearly always too much for any one person to do it well. You are going to need to hire an engineering manager, a product manager, a program manager, a project manager, or some combination of all four. For brevity, let's call this person a PM.

PM hires are the most critical hires you can make. Hiring the wrong person to be a PM on your team more than sucks—it's like jabbing a salted knife into the collective kidney of your engineering team on a daily basis. The wrong person can change the product direction for the worse, hide information from you, delay tasks that would otherwise be done poorly but quickly, and will cause great angst within an engineering team. Needless to say, hire carefully, and err on the side of not hiring a PM.

If you need to hire a PM, you should start by defining the role you're hiring someone to perform. Generally in the software industry, there are program managers, product managers, project managers, and engineering managers. The actual definition of each role varies based on the company, but the following sections give some guidelines on how the roles differ.

PROGRAM MANAGERS

I once interviewed for a program manager role at Microsoft that I ultimately declined. During my interview I was asked, "What does a PM do?" That this would even be an interview question speaks to the difficulty of the job! My answer? "A PM ships software."

More specifically, a program manager focuses on integrating different teams and job functions. Josh Herst, the CEO of Walk Score and a former venture partner at Madrona Venture Group, once said, "Program management is a glue-and-grease role. You pull disparate functions together so that the machine can work and then grease the machine to make it work better."

Another way to look at program management is that it is a technical role with less business focus than product management and less project focus than project management. The deliverables a program manager will produce are therefore more ambiguous than some other roles and the focus on "glue and grease" is manifest.

PRODUCT MANAGERS

Product managers traditionally focus more on the business side of software. There are even product managers who don't work on software. These product managers are typically MBAs who focus on brand management, pricing, go-to-market strategies, and so on. Your software product manager will do these jobs and will help prioritize feature development by attempting to speak with the voice of the customer.

Product managers at Google do pretty much everything but write code. That said, I know of more than one product manager (including myself) who wrote code while at Google. Product managers at Facebook and the newer Bay Area startups tend to have the same responsibilities, mainly because the startups and Facebook seem to be largely staffed by ex-Googlers.

PROJECT MANAGERS

Project managers, or technical program managers as they're known at Google, focus primarily on the schedule and coordinating team efforts. They ask for estimates, they identify dependencies, and they figure out how to get more done in less time. Want to know if having great project management chops is worthwhile? In 2007, a truck carrying 8,600 gallons of gasoline crashed on the ramp connecting I-80 to I-580 in California, destroying a major artery and sending local traffic into a state of intense disarray.[1] Initial estimates to repair the damage exceeded $10 million, but gutsy C. C. Myers, Inc., came in with a bid of just less than $900,000—and a clause that said they'd be paid a $200,000 per-day bonus for every day they came in ahead of schedule. Given that the state was estimating an economic loss of $6 million per day, this seemed like a good deal to California. The C. C. Myers crew, through a combination of brilliant project management and good old hard work, beat the target date by a full month, earning a 500% ($5 million) bonus.

---

1   *http://en.wikipedia.org/wiki/MacArthur_Maze*

ENGINEERING MANAGERS

Engineering managers are frequently coders grown older. The best "eng managers" are those who have been promoted into the role because they love their teams, understand people, know how to ship, and want to build brilliant products. The worst are those frustrated engineers who only wanted more control and more money. You know who you are. Cut it out.

Engineering managers may or may not have product managers, program managers, project managers, or even technical program managers working for or with them. Some engineering managers see their primary role as maintaining the happiness of the engineering team. Others see it as maintaining engineering quality through hiring, process, and other tools. Still others see their role as similar to a product manager, but with access to the engineering resources to build the stuff they want to build.

Every engineering team will have an engineering manager, but not every team will have a product, program, or project manager. Therefore, if you have one of these other titles you must partner well with your engineering manager, because if your engineering team is unhappy, unskilled, or lacks a quality process, you'll have a very hard time shipping. Similarly, if you're an engineering manager, finding people who can support your weaknesses and enable you to ship faster and better is very important.

HOW TO HIRE A PRODUCT, PROGRAM, OR ENGINEERING MANAGER

Hiring leads for a team is very hard. I believe that Google, Amazon, Microsoft, and similar companies are terrible at finding great leads through the interview process; you can see this in how candidates are evaluated. For example, at Google some of the strongest inputs into hiring decisions are the candidate's GPA, the schools he or she attended, and internal referrals. None of these factors is part of the interview process, which should tell you something. At Amazon, candidates must be very technical, but the questions they're asked are trivial to answer with a little studying (more on this in Chapter 9). I think that the process of hiring leads is largely broken, but it's a major part of your job as a lead, so you need to know how to do it. There are five major rules for hiring leads:

- Hire people who are smarter than you.
- Hire people who understand they are not the boss.
- Hire people with clear, data-driven communications practices.
- Hire people who are quantitative.
- Hire people with gumption.

Hire people who are smarter than you

First, you should hire people who are smarter than you. However, Mike Smith, a former Google GPM who used to coordinate product management hiring in the Seattle/Kirkland Google offices, says, "This statement ignores basic human instincts...[you want] to exert control." Therefore, you must hire only people who are smarter than you if you are willing to empower them and trust them to be team leads in their own right. I honestly believe Eric Schmidt both espoused and lived to this principle. I heard him say, "Thank you for ignoring me; that's why we hired you." Sadly, he said this about someone else—I didn't have the guts to ignore Eric because he was really much, much smarter than I. Someone else hired me; that's how I got hired. If you can hire people who are smarter than you and empower them to ignore you, read on. Otherwise, don't hire anyone. Just do the job yourself.

Since you've decided to hire team leads who are smarter than you, you're going to want to know how to assess brains. I triple-dislike the Microsoft approach to asking "brain teaser"–type questions because I think they don't actually test smarts. For example, here's a real question I was asked during an interview at Microsoft:

> Q: You're in a boat, and you're holding a big rock. You throw the rock into the lake. What happens to the level of the lake?
> A: It goes down because the rock in the water displaces only the volume of the rock, rather than the volume of water equivalent to the mass of the rock, which is what happens in the boat.
> Q: <long pause> Wait, had you heard this before?
> A: No, but I studied engineering...?

The only interesting part of candidates' responses to a question of this nature is what happens to them if they get stuck. It is a good sign if the candidate can get unstuck without help. Beyond that, people's ability to think their way through a brain teaser has little to do with their ability to get to root cause, measure their business well, or think about competitive markets. Please don't ask these kinds of questions.

To those of you saying, "Yes, but what if the stone was pumice and could, in fact, float?" I say, you're missing the point.

The best way to test raw smarts is by checking references. Ram Charan, coauthor of *Execution: The Discipline of Getting Things Done* (Crown Business), makes it a point to check his candidate's references personally. Great PM managers I know do the same thing. If it's too early in the process to check references, the candidate's résumé is a good enough proxy. A strong GPA at great schools is an additional predictor of success in the role, but it is not the only indicator.

Substantial launches with real deliverables is a key indicator of success; after all, if we're trying to achieve shipping greatness, a history of shipping should count for a lot. A leadership candidate who has a long, wishy-washy résumé is almost certainly a no-hire, but a lead with a single-page résumé that highlights product releases and their monetary or user impact is a "must interview" candidate.

OK, so you're not yet convinced. You're ready to present the classic heavy-marble problem (find the heavy marble out of 23 otherwise equally weighted marbles with just a balance) or some variant of it. Let me help you out. *Potential candidates listen up*: the answer to this and all questions in this class is a binary search. It is $\log N$ K fast, where N is 2 for splitting the marbles in half and 3 if you use three piles.

Now go ask for the candidate's GPA, check references, and don't ask any more silly questions.

Look for candidates who understand that they are not the boss

You should hire people who can be Not-The-Boss even if you are hiring an engineering people manager. You want your engineering team to do what they think is right and lean on the engineering manager for support, not orders. The only way to know that a PM understands the Not-The-Boss requirement is by meeting with the candidate face-to-face.

When I interview a candidate face-to-face, I pose a question I borrowed from McKinsey and Company: "Tell me about a time when you changed someone's mind, and what techniques you used." I listen for information about how the candidate responded to not being in charge. I look for evidence of collaborative decision making (see Chapter 11). I look for data-based arguments (see Chapter 6) and smart escalation (see Chapter 11 again). If the candidate says, "Well, I just convinced the tech lead to try it," that's a good indicator that this lead is used to being the boss.

Look for clear, data-driven, and specific communications

Here's an example of what happens when you hire a bad communicator:

Me: Is \<redacted> done?
\<redacted also>@amazon.com: Yeah.

Me: Like, tested and running?

<redacted also>@amazon.com: Oh, no, but it looks mostly like Java.

True story! I need real, concrete answers from leads, so when I ask a specific follow-up question, such as "How did you convince Larry to approve your launch?" a bad answer is "We talked about it, and he kind of came around." A great answer is:

> First, I scheduled a meeting with the stakeholders to get them onboard. Next, I had my SVP send a note. After Larry was presold with that note, I had a 10-slide deck that I presented to Larry and we listened to his feedback. We were able to address his concerns in that meeting and moved forward.

Note that this latter answer is brief. It is specific. It has a beginning and an end. It speaks to what the individual did and also to how the individual worked as part of a team.

Hire quantitatively inclined candidates

A good technical leader should be able to do math on his or her feet. Candidates who use numbers, even when referring to the number of slides they had, get good marks from me. I occasionally ask candidates market-sizing questions, but my goal is not to assess if they can segment a market, but rather to see if they can make good approximations and do math on their feet. A typical market-sizing question might be "What's the market for a new smartphone in the US?" Most MBAs can answer this type of question in their sleep, as they practice them before they go out for consulting interviews. Here's how I'd answer the new smartphone market-size question (I doubt the answer is right, but you can see how it demonstrates that I'm not afraid of numbers):

> There are 350 million people in the US. I estimate that of those 350 million people, folks between 12 and 75 have need for a mobile phone. That's probably a total US mobile market of about 300 million users, give or take.
>
> Now, the market for smartphones is different. Let's segment the market into callers, social media users, and business users.
>
> Social media is most dominant from 12–30, so that's about 30% of the market: 90 million. Add to that estimate the business users, who are, say, 50% of the 30–60 market, and you get 50% of an additional 30%.

Half of 90 million is 45 million, so that's an additional 45 million users, for a total of 135 million users. Let's put the remainder of those 300 million users into callers—we don't care about them right now.

So 135 million might want a smartphone. I think Apple is planning on shipping 20 million iPhone 5s out of the gate, and Android will be double that, so it checks out roughly right.

If we are introducing a new phone, we probably are selling to two major groups: new smartphone users and upgraders. So, if you assume that there are probably 40 million iPhones and 80 million Android phones, that's 120 million smartphones deployed, leaving 15 million as new users. Of the 120 million phones, figure a three-year upgrade cycle—that's conservative. So, one-third of those 120 million will upgrade in a year. That's 40 million.

In other words, I think you have a potential market of 55 million phones in your first year—40 million upgraders and 15 million new users. Now, how many phones you sell is a very different story! Isn't this mobile business fascinating, how fast it is growing?

That is how you answer a market-sizing question. Start by making a numerical assumption. Check your assumptions with other data as you go along. Use round numbers and whittle down your estimate using rational market segmentation. Arrive at a real number. Finally, show your enthusiasm, even though you probably don't want to work at a company that asks this type of question.

Hire people with gumption

Leaders are frequently the driving force behind your team, and if they don't bring energy with them your cause is lost. If one goal of your mission statement is to inspire (see Chapter 1), the person who delivers the mission best would be inspirational, and inspiration comes from energy. One sign of good energy that you might be able to see in an interview is a novel idea, because candidates who are willing to invest a lot of energy thinking beyond your specific question are likely to do so with their own team. I also look for excitement around problem solving. The design problems I ask are all very interesting to me; great candidates get excited about the problem with me and can explore the problem space.

How to Acquire a Company

It's not unusual for larger companies to acquire a smaller company at the initial phase of the project. It's a prebaked team, isn't it? It's also not unusual for a software project leader to seek out potential acquisitions in order to solve a problem or get to market faster. Acquisitions are rarely easy, so it's important to know how to handle them properly.

There are generally four reasons why you might consider acquiring a company.

Intellectual property

You can use the technology, content, or patents that the company built.

Talent

You can use the people the company hired.

Customers

You can use the company's customers to accelerate the growth of your business.

Defense

You're buying the company so somebody else can't.

Of these four reasons, Mike Smith, a VP of engineering at Disney who has experience with acquisitions at Disney and Microsoft, says, "Hope to get two out of the four. Expect one. If you're being sold on more than two, nine times out of ten you're going to be disappointed."

INTELLECTUAL PROPERTY ACQUISITIONS

Before you even consider acquiring technology or content, you need to do the basic math of build versus buy. The math is truly basic: how many engineers for how many months will it take to build, test, and ship similar software? Multiply this number of engineering months by the cost of a fully loaded engineer for a month. Subtract the cost—measured again in units of engineering person months—of integrating the company's intellectual property. The result is how much you should be willing to pay, assuming time to market is not critical.

However, time to market is always critical, so do some more rough math to figure out what the value of potential sales is if you are selling your software after the acquisition and integration is complete and before you would otherwise ship your own software. Or, pick six months' sales because that's probably equivalent to the revenue you may gain. Add this figure to your first estimate, and you'll have the full value of the deal.

If you think that you can get to a deal for a number less than what you just computed, then it's reasonable to move forward.

Next, you need to look carefully at the software you will acquire. You can't trust that the company's code is good. Well, maybe you can trust that it's good, but you need to verify that it is. You need to get a senior engineer from your team who will not work with the business in the future to review the code. Startups get very twitchy about exposing their secret sauce, and your lawyers are going to get worried about "tainting" your team if the deal doesn't go through. But there's no help for it. You must have someone whom you and your team trust review the code and architecture. If you don't, you're buying a rental car without taking it to a mechanic first.

If you've reviewed the code and it looks OK, make sure you can put together a plan to integrate the team and the technology. Like most projects, the integration project will take longer than you expect. Unlike most projects, however, it will take *much* longer than you expect because you have new people, foreign servers, different software licenses, and all sorts of undocumented details to deal with.

TALENT ACQUISITIONS

Talent acquisitions are the trickiest of all acquisitions. This is not surprising, since they're all about people and people can be tricky. You must evaluate people like you normally do: interview them. The more people you interview, the lower your acquisition risk will be, because you have more complete information. Conversely, the more people you interview, the more you disrupt both businesses. You must conduct your interviews carefully.

A caveat here: don't interview people without them knowing that it's an interview. I know of at least one case in which this happened, and it backfired. The deal team ended up redoing all of the interviews, and it soured the deal.

Interviews will also help you understand where the employees fit into your organization. I use three core buckets for talent:

Key individuals

> These are the people who keep the lights on, and without them, you'd have to backfill immediately. They might be hard to backfill because their domain knowledge is so deep.

Good hires

> These are people you'd happily hire into your current business. They are A-class candidates, but you could also spend a few months hiring on your own and land a similar candidate.

Surplus talent

> These are employees who don't meet your hiring bar, so you're going to do one of two things with them: a) put them on contract for a period so you can transition them out, or b) terminate their employment. This may seem like a hard transition, but this is the reality of acquisitions.

Talent acquisitions of more than a few people are very hard because of the process, the interviewing, and the subjectivity of the deal valuation. They can also be very difficult to integrate. Mike Smith shares a frightening anecdote from his time at Microsoft:

> I drove the acquisition of a company called Conversagent (to be Microsoft Windows Live agents). In evaluating the talent, it was clear that there was a good need to hire between 20–30 additional engineers to get the scale that met the business needs. The acquisition was approved with that constraint, but then finance decided that it would sit on releasing the headcount to be hired against. For 9 months. Core talent left at 12 months, with no backfill. The acquisition failed and is now worth less than a tenth of its purchase value.

This story shows how important it is to get all parties, including HR, legal, and finance, bought into your talent acquisition before you close the deal.

CUSTOMER BASE ACQUISITIONS

If you make $2 per user over the lifetime of that user and you're going to acquire a company with 10 million users, you should be able to make $20 million bucks, right? Wrong. You're only going to make a fraction of that. What fraction you make depends on what you do with the business.

If the business you intend to acquire is self-sustaining, you can keep it running largely as is and attempt to upsell those customers to your new product. However, you'll probably have a pretty low take rate. If your take rate on those 10 million users is about 20%, the deal is worth less than $4 million.

If you plan to shut down the business and convert its users into your own, you will likely pay substantial costs to shutter the business and you'll lose customers along the way. You might estimate that a deal done this way is worth about 50% of the potential value, or approximately $5 million.

Because these numbers are so low, you're most likely to look at a customer acquisition deal as a sales accelerator for situations in which there's a highly competitive market and getting big fast matters. If you're in one of those businesses, you might want to get out now before the stress kills you. Or at least switch to Tylenol, because your stomach will thank you. Assuming you don't get out, you're going to value this deal by estimating your sales increases, which is highly speculative math.

No matter how you value this deal, make sure that you're using the right baseline data. That means looking at logs. Look at not just impressions and signed-up users, but "seven-day active" user counts. You're after repeat customers, so you want to measure returning users and engagement (time spent on the site or using the app). Have your team review the log data, or at least understand the systems that are generating the reports, whether those are Webtrends or Google Analytics.

DEFENSIVE ACQUISITIONS

I have not led a defensive deal. In my opinion, they're not very nice and smell of fear-based decision making. If you have the pockets to do a defensive deal, please don't be evil when you do one.

If you're even considering doing a defensive deal, you probably need to think about what monopolistic practices are. "I'm not a lawyer" is the first thing you should get used to saying because at least your comments will be in context. I'm not a lawyer, so I won't tell you what not to do.

GOTCHAS AND BEST PRACTICES WITH ACQUISITIONS

Here are some final tips and warnings to keep in mind when you're considering acquiring another company.

Plan to embed part of your team into their team

Embedding some of your senior staff into the acquired team works great because it brings the culture, practices, and policies of your business into the new team. In addition, a good, scrappy development lead will unblock the new team and help them be much more efficient more quickly. Your new team will be more likely to be happy as a result, because they will be productive, and productivity breeds happiness. You should budget approximately 1 senior engineer for every 10 acquired engineers. If you don't have anyone you can spare, then you need to look for ways to pull talent off of the new team and use them to backfill this dev lead so he or she can join the new team. It's that important.

Don't underestimate the importance of culture fit and the time it takes new people to figure out how to operate under your unique brand of insanity. To do so is to create an unruly group of engineers who are biding their time until the one-year mark is up and they can cash out their options. That's a miserable way for those people to work, and it's bad for the rest of your business. Make sure you get the new company well integrated into your old company. Embedding your best engineers into the new team is a great way to help this.

Plan to integrate the product

You need to know not only how you're going to stick their servers behind your virtual IP, but also what you're going to do with their brand and how their billing systems will work with your billing systems. Many acquisitions are less successful than they could be because the acquirer ends up paying a multiyear engineering cost to integrate the business. A clear plan makes transitions easier for teams, too.

Understand all the prior deals and liabilities

It's always a bummer to discover late in the game that the founder owes someone a million bucks. It's not your problem, but for some reason, founders always want you to take care of them, so it becomes your problem. Having a good conversation about debts, liabilities, and any deals the company might have signed before you reach a number is very important. A good attorney will help you with this, but it's best to do your own homework, too.

How to Work with Offshore or Remote Teams

It's pretty hard to work with a good engineering team in the best of times. It's very difficult to work with a team that's in another office. It's approaching impossible if you add a 12-hour time difference to the equation. The situation is basically hilarious when you try to coordinate across mutually exclusive time zones like Sydney, Stockholm, India, and the West Coast of the US. I've led these kinds of distributed projects, and I'm giggling still.

Remote—or "distributed" in Google vernacular—teams are a necessary evil at this stage of software development. One reason you will use remote teams is that areas are known for their specialties and acquire like-minded geniuses. For example, Tel Aviv and Stockholm have video gurus. Romania has security geeks. Big distributed-systems brains tend to come from college towns like Pittsburgh and Seattle. More than 50% of Google's employees work outside the home office of Mountain View. Facebook, Google, Ticketmaster, and an increasingly large number of Bay Area companies have all opened offices in Seattle, just as one example. US Immigration has made it difficult for some of the world's top engineering talent to work *from* the US—but not *for* the US.

Given these industry trends, and your near-infinite need for brilliant engineering talent, you're going to encounter a time when you think about working with engineers outside your hometown. It will be challenging, but there are some things you can do to make your life easier. Nine things, in fact:

- Don't rent an engineer—build an engineering team.
- Overcommunicate.
- Do not outsource design or PM roles.
- Adapt to cultural differences.
- Build clear requirements.
- Suck up the time difference and meet anyway.
- Establish great leads.
- Travel a lot or barely at all.
- Drink with the remote team.

DON'T RENT AN ENGINEER—BUILD AN ENGINEERING TEAM

Engineering projects are long term and complex, and benefit substantially from peer collaboration. The best way to embrace and leverage these dynamics is by building a team of at least three engineers who all share a charter. Three engineers amounts to what I call "critical mass," meaning there are enough people that the team can power itself. The charter gives the team a sense of direction. It also helps the team make decisions autonomously, which is something you need when you have less direct oversight. For example, when a developer finishes one project or gets stuck, the charter helps inform what he or she works on next. Defining a clear charter for the team also helps them feel less anxious about their future.

OVERCOMMUNICATE

There's a truism I've noticed working with remote teams: the farther the team is from you, the more anxious they are. If you're based in California, for example, New York will only assume something was miscommunicated, get on a plane, fly to California, and complain loudly. Even the best engineering teams in Sydney and India, on the other hand, straight-up panic. They're so far away from the States that they assume they're misunderstood, underappreciated, and kept out of the loop. The best thing you can do to ameliorate these feelings is to overcommunicate.

Use Skype, Google+ Hangouts, WebEx, and generally anything you can get your hands on to increase the quality of your communication with your remote teams. Because developers hate using telephones, reducing initiation friction is really important. One team I had at Google was split between Seattle and Mountain View. We bought small, dedicated video-conference units for each team so that we could quickly call the other team in for daily standups or random design discussions. This worked really well. You can do the same thing through Google+'s Hangouts With Extras.

TRY VERY HARD NOT TO OUTSOURCE DESIGN
OR PM ROLES

It's possible to make outsourced design work well, but you are leaving huge value behind on the table. A great designer will fix a multitude of problems you didn't even know you had, and can do this best when he or she has full visibility into everything you're doing. You can find more information on how to work with designers in Chapter 3. Do everything you can to hire someone internally and outsource only visual design.

Similar to designers, product, program, and project managers benefit hugely from being immersed in the team. For example, they may overhear snippets of conversations that expose miscommunication. They discover areas where engineering teams are blocked. They repeat your mission and strategy so that the team stays aligned. They build personal relationships with the engineering team that enable engineers to feel comfortable making task-size estimates. For these reasons and many more, I can't imagine outsourcing a product, program, or project manager role.

APPRECIATE CULTURAL DIFFERENCES

I went through an eye-opening personal performance review cycle once. I worked closely with a female engineer who did fantastic work. We'll call her Sarah so you can't track her down. Sarah showed strong leadership and wrote great code, and I thought she had wonderful ideas and we made great product progress. I was a huge supporter of her promotion case. You know how this is going to end, right?

Sarah's engineering director and I sat down one day, and he told me I had a problem. Sarah didn't feel like I was listening to her. I was stunned. And this very smart Chinese-American engineering director explained something to me. He said, to paraphrase, "You should take into account two things: Sarah's a woman, and she's a Chinese-American woman. She has a lot of experience not being heard and not being able to speak up. And you're a 6'4" white guy who talks really loud."

Cultural differences are fascinating. I certainly shouldn't treat or evaluate Sarah any differently because of her race or gender—that would be dumb, evil, and illegal. But in a parallel situation, where I'm working with a big white guy from Romania who has a weaker grasp of English than he has of C++, I might well choose not to use all my Ivy League words. That's just good sense, and it might make sense to adjust the way I communicate for the unique audience that Sarah represents.

This is only one example of a cultural difference. I could go on and on. For example, I've seen teams in Zurich be far more concerned, compared to US teams, about getting to a "right" solution than getting a prototype built. My local team in Seattle found this infuriating. But when the Seattle team understood that this was the Zurich team's approach and it would be OK in the long run, it helped us give the Swiss the space they needed.

You do not need to understand how each and every culture uniquely works, but rather to recognize that teams on the East Coast of the US are going to behave differently than teams on the West Coast, and teams on the West Coast are going to behave differently than teams in the UK. You must actively work to understand where you may have differences and then compensate. You can start understanding these differences by over-communicating and looking for patterns in reactions.

BUILD CLEAR REQUIREMENTS

New teams have some similarities regardless of where they are located. One such similarity is that they don't really know what they're supposed to do or why they're supposed to do it. Remote teams are the worst, though, because they don't have you sitting in the middle of their office answering offhand questions, repeating your mission to investors on the phone 10 times per day, and harassing your development lead about how critical your next deadline is. Since you're not there, you need to provide a "virtual you" in the form of bulletproof requirements. If you do a good job with the product requirements document described in Chapter 2, you'll be in good shape. While great requirements are critical for all teams, they are even more necessary for remote teams.

SUCK UP THE TIME DIFFERENCE

A 12-hour time difference stinks, but there's nothing you can do about it. You have to absorb it in some way, because you need to have status meetings and one-on-ones, and sometimes you just need to take a half-hour of your life to listen to someone talk about his or her life. That half-hour isn't for you, it's for the other person, and it can be a bummer when you'd rather be watching *The Daily Show*.

I've only come up with two ways to cope with this problem:

- Get a TiVo.
- Work early mornings or late evenings, but don't work both. Whichever works better for you, set up your meetings to always happen at the beginning or end of your day.

That's all I have. You just have to suck it up. Communication and face time are important, and it's easy to skip them when the timing is hard, so pay attention to how you spend your time and invest in your remote teams.

ESTABLISH GREAT LEADS

You may try to be everywhere at once, but you are only going to end up being at a few places, and you'll probably be there late. Being a little ball of stress doesn't help anyone, and the scotch you're drinking to mellow out isn't good for your liver. You need lieutenants in your remote locations. If you can, ship one of your best leads from your home office over to the new team for a month or so. Sending a great technical leader to embed with the team is a great way of transplanting culture and process, which is why I recommend it for acquired teams.

Establishing a local lead will eliminate at least a couple of late-night meetings for you, because that local lead will meet one-on-one with your home office engineering lead. Not only do these meetings help reduce the volume of technical conversations you participate in and increase space for cultural conversation, but they can also help reduce the time required to discover a crisis. For example, if you meet with the remote office on Monday, and your home office engineering lead meets on Thursday, your home office engineering lead may discover the crisis two whole developer days faster than you would have, because your meeting wasn't scheduled until Monday.

TRAVEL A LOT OR NOT AT ALL

If you talk to frequent travelers, you'll learn that if you travel every other week, it gets easier. Traveling is still rotten, but it's better, because you fly better classes, your bags stay packed, and your mileage status gets you through security faster. You stay at the same hotel consistently, and as a result you lose things less frequently. You learn how to eat well on the road and have a harder time avoiding the gym in the hotel.

The other simple travel trick is the one-day turnaround. I know it sounds crazy—go out and come back the same day—but it has great benefits for flights shorter than three hours. You sleep in your own bed. You don't change clothes. You catch up on email on the plane. Ultimately, you'll find something that works, but if you can convince yourself to get up crazy-early, you may find you like it more than you like hotel room coffee.

Traveling a significant distance every month or two just stinks. You would think that it's less frequent and therefore better, but in many ways it's worse.

DRINK WITH THE REMOTE TEAM

I once spent some time in Korea pitching a major consumer electronics company on an opportunity to build some service-specific hardware. My business development colleague, Jake, and I went out to dinner with their biz guy and their engineering guy, who told us a fascinating story.

Many Koreans drink this vodka-like alcohol called soju. I did my best to like it, and anyway, I was sufficiently jet-lagged that I lacked the judgment to not drink it. The engineering guy proceeded to tell us that in Korea, many engineers have strong feelings but feel that they can't express them in the workplace. In fact, the reason why the Korean engineers enjoy the soju so much is that they can go out with their coworkers after work, drink this stuff, and say what's really on their minds.

The lesson here is that, in addition to respecting cultural differences, you should understand that different environments can expose different truths. Bars and restaurants are two of them (two of the best, if you ask me) and are enabled by alcohol.

It's important to note that you don't need to be a big drinker to have beer help you. While there may be some international protocol around business drinking, your engineering team is probably happy to drink around a teetotaler. They really want you to let them drink and tell you want they want. Oh, and they want you to pick up the tab, too.

How to Join a New Team

Regardless of whether you have built a new team or were dropped from a high altitude into a train wreck to sort things out, you're going to need to do two critical things: figure out what role you should play, and make the right first moves.

It's critical that you figure out what your ideal role on this specific team should be. Some engineering teams don't want any project management—in which case, you need to figure out how to do as little as possible but still track your project. Some engineering teams want you to focus on marketing, while others will invite you into technical discussions and will welcome your input if you're sufficiently deep technically.

To figure out what your role on the team should be, you must be sensitive to what the team needs. You can check the pulse of the team through one-on-one weekly meetings with the team's other leaders. Build relationships by meeting monthly one-on-one with each engineer on your team just to touch base. It's also important to drive transparency into all your processes so you build trust. These actions will enable you to focus on doing things that only you can do and being a great servant to your team. They are also investments that will pay off during the challenging sprint to the finish.

There is one unique hiccup you might encounter at this point. It's happened to me only once, but it was painful. You may figure out what the team needs and wants, but find that you're not empowered to do what you need to in order to ship greatness. This could be because you're being micromanaged, or because you've tried and there's strong resistance to change, or a host of other reasons. Some of these problems are solvable, like teams being resistant to change. Others, like having leaders marginalize the job you believe needs to be done, are less solvable. When you hit a situation like this, you might consider joining a different team.

If you plan to stay on the team now that you have a sense of what to focus on, and you've gathered a little information about the team, its project, and its problems, you've probably discovered that the product, program, or project is a mess. Half of the time, all three look like zombie leftovers. It doesn't matter how good the engineering team is, most projects look like a disaster when you show up.

If, for some bizarre reason, you show up and everything looks clean and happy, check again, and then start saving your pennies so you can buy your options. But you're probably like most of us. You've got a mess on your hands, and you need to do two important things right away.

First, don't tell the team that the product is a mess! They probably don't think the situation is a mess and won't take kindly to you calling it out. Trust me on this—you don't want to learn this lesson the hard way. Remember that they've been working on this longer than you, and that there are many reasons why the product is a mess. The odds are pretty good that the engineers on the team are reasonably smart, so there's a good chance that there's a leadership problem. More often than not, the leadership problem is a lack of leadership, which is why it's good that you joined the team. When there is a leadership problem, escalate.

I'm a pretty straightforward guy, so early in my career I embraced the notion of "speaking truth to power." This led me to cheerfully and directly point out the problems I saw in some teams. Even when I did this pointing as delicately as I could (which is not very delicately, unfortunately), it was not well received. I was an outsider and I clearly didn't understand that "we do things differently on <foo>; you need to spend more time ramping up." In some circumstances, like when I drilled into the work of a group of designers on Google Maps, I caused real turmoil and pain. I've learned that in most circumstances it's best to work from the inside out whenever possible, so don't tell the team that the product is a mess.

The second thing you must do upon discovering a mess is make a choice: you can slip your date and fix the mess, or you can suck it up and ship. The best time to slip your ship date is right when you join the team. Because you are new, you're not responsible for the slip; you're just pointing out that the team's not going to make the date. If you make your case with objective data like bug counts, engineering estimates, and vacation schedules, you can have a dispassionate conversation about the ship date.

On the other hand, sometimes you've been brought in to ship at all costs, and that's what you must do. Freshness and improvements matter to users, so this makes some sense. Make sure that you don't have massive privacy or security bugs, and then force the software out the door. Fix the team and process problems when you can build on the success of having shipped. Sack the lame-o's later when you have the time to work them through a reasonable PIP (performance improvement plan) process and give them a chance.

In my experience, there are five major types of teams you will join. In each situation there's a best way to react. Table 8-1 shows how you can identify the teams by what they say and suggests good responses you can give.

Table 8-1. Team types and reactions

What they say	What you say
Shiny Ball! Let's build 100 features!	How about V2? Let's focus on a single story for V1.
We've been screwed 100 times, you're 101.	I know things are rough. Let's craft a really short-term plan that we all believe in and sell it, and go from there.
We know what we're doing. Why are you here?	I'm here to do some business stuff and help you manage up. We'll figure out other things over time *(and then work through the leads to drive change)*.
Well, our boss didn't tell us about this.	Let's all get together with the boss and get on the same page.
We're having a good time. We made these fun demos!	Sounds good. *(...and go talk to senior management. There's no point in asking a team that's happily playing catch to win the World Series unless that's actually the stated goal.)*
Thank God you're here.	You're welcome. What did the last person do that helped you so much?

9

How to Build Great, Shippable Technology

IF YOU WANT TO ship a great product quickly, you must be able to ask insightful questions, provide good directional guidance, and make smart technical decisions about what you must build now and what you can build later. You must also be able to evaluate and hire engineering managers. Therefore, you must understand your technology at least as well as you understand the oil in your car. You know the oil doesn't make the car go, but you also know that you had better keep it filled up or your Dodge Dart will become an oversized doorstop. That's all you really need to know to get home.

While you need to be technical enough to address these issues, I believe you don't need a computer science degree to achieve shipping greatness. You can achieve shipping greatness if you understand the systems approach I take in this chapter. In fact, I'm convinced that if you understand these things, you can coast gracefully through the technical part of a lead-level interview at Google, Amazon, or Microsoft. If you want to ace an interview or gracefully handle a product development process, you need to know the four S's: *servers*, *services*, *speed*, and *scaling*. Once you understand these four basic elements, you'll be able to ask your team the right questions.

The First S: Servers

Don't buy servers if you can help it. First, you'll have to learn a lot about servers, and anything you learn will be obsolete in six months, which is frustrating and inefficient. Second, you'll have to do tons of maintenance, like applying service packs, installing upgrades, and performing other tedious chores. What's even more frustrating about specifying and maintaining your own servers is that your engineering team will frequently have to do the work. It's not what they're best at, because they've learned the same lesson I just gave you: anything they learn about servers is obsolete in six months, so the good engineers try to learn how to avoid maintenance chores.

Save yourself a headache and the bottle of scotch you'll inevitably have to buy a surly dev to make up for the late-night trip to the network operations center—use a hosted solution. Use Amazon's EC2 or Google's AppEngine or a similar service. You'll give up a lot of control you didn't want anyway, and you'll save yourself a lot of pain.

If you must have your own systems for some strange reason, then lease them through a provider. Don't worry about where the provider is located. Instead, worry about whether you can get someone technical on the phone when the virtual IP goes haywire. How will you know if the virtual IP has gone haywire, since you didn't complete that PhD in CS? The properly selected provider will have a proper engineer on staff. If it doesn't, it's your fault—you picked the wrong vendor. Always check references (see Chapter 8 on how to build a team for more on this).

Your systems will typically have a three-tier architecture, as shown in Figure 9-1. This architecture may sound complicated, but it is actually dirt simple.

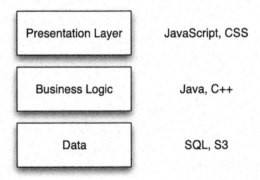

Figure 9-1. A simple, three-tier architecture

The data layer is typically a database where your data lives—things like customer records and so forth. You'll retrieve the data using some kind of syntax that is similar to SQL (Structured Query Language). If you've ever used Microsoft Access at a moderately advanced level, you've encountered SQL.

The business logic is the brains of your operation. It's where all the tricky calculations happen and where the IF {Charlie said no;} THEN {kill Charlie;} type statements go. Your engineers will build this in Java or C++ or something similar.

The presentation layer is generally HTML and JavaScript. It formats the output of your business logic so the data looks pretty. JavaScript allows users to interact in real time.

AJAX (Asynchronous JavaScript and XML) is nothing more than allowing JavaScript to submit mini-page requests to your business logic, rather than requiring the user to submit a whole form. Instead of the server returning HTML and JavaScript, it returns just a tiny bit of data in the form of XML. So AJAX has nothing to do with a three-tier architecture.

It is possible to flatten this three-tier architecture into two tiers and allow your engineering team to write one file that contains both business logic and presentation logic. Shudder to think. Some frameworks will even hook up with databases in such a way that the database can return XML that can be used directly by frontend JavaScript! These and other great time savers are lovely initially but will haunt you for years after, just like that bad job you did on the grout in the shower. They're great for internal projects but will probably not survive the sale of your business.

The Second S: Services

A *service-oriented architecture* (SOA) doesn't have much to do with a three-tier architecture—but you had better believe you want one! An SOA breaks down the middle tier that contains your business logic into a collection of independent services. These services may run on the same server, but they are built, versioned, and run independently. Figure 9-2 shows an example SOA.

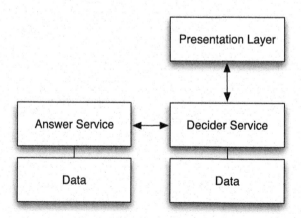

Figure 9-2. A system architecture organized around services

In the SOA shown in Figure 9-2, your engineering team will put the system that figures out Charlie's response into the answer service. The logic for deciding what to do with Charlie's answer lives in the decider service.

These services are connected through *application programming interfaces* (APIs). While not identical, for your purposes these are the same as *remote procedure calls* (RPCs). So don't let anyone fool you: APIs and RPCs enable a service to talk to another service. The decider asks the answer service, "What's Charlie's answer?" though an API. That API might look like this:

```
whatIsTheAnswer(Charlie)
```

The answer service returns an answer to the decider, which can choose what to do with Charlie. These are the kinds of APIs you want to write into your product requirements document. The boundaries of which bits of your system should be in which service aren't particularly important. In fact, you can even use services outside your company, like a credit card processor to clear transactions or Amazon's S3 to store data. What is important is that your system is fast and scalable.

If you want a fast system, avoid service chaining at all costs. I know you'd just convinced yourself that services were going to save the world (Amazon certainly did when I was there!), but look at the SOA in Figure 9-3.

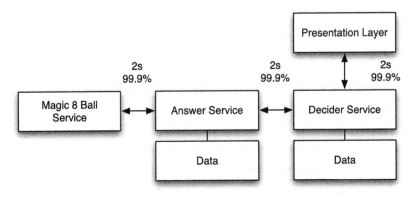

Figure 9-3. An SOA with service chaining

In Figure 9-3, we've decided to outsource some of our answers, the ones we really care about, to a new Magic 8 Ball service. Since you're so passionate about speed and believe that users will leave if you don't provide a response to the user in two seconds or less, you've convinced the engineering team to meet a two-second 99.9% *service-level agreement* (SLA). Your SLA means that only one out of a thousand responses takes more than two seconds. That's pretty good, right?

It would be fine if performance were dependent only on the Magic 8 Ball service. Unfortunately, the decider depends on the answer service, which also has a two-second SLA. Therefore, some users are going to have to wait up to six seconds to get a response, because they have to wait for each service in the chain to return a result. What's worse, most of these systems deliver responses in a normal distribution, meaning you're probably looking at an average response time of nearly two seconds to the user—on *average*, not at the peak. Never chain services if you can help it. Look for alternatives.

DRAWBACKS TO SERVICE-ORIENTED ARCHITECTURES (SOAs)

Steve Yegge, a staff software engineer at Google and a former senior engineer at Amazon, wrote a terrific rant about why Amazon's internal SOA is profoundly better than Google's collection of more disorganized systems. He points out a few things to pay attention to:

- When you have a lot of services and the customer sees a problem, you may have to trace the customer-facing problem through many services before you find the one service that's responsible. Good monitoring can help mitigate this problem.
- Interteam dependencies become more of an issue, and if a team fails to tell you that they're changing their API, they can easily break your system. Each team must therefore maintain backward compatibility and communicate to consumers proactively, which is hard.
- It's hard to build a great *sandbox*, or testing environment, because every one of your systems must exist in that sandbox so that you don't pollute production systems with garbage data. Even if you do have every one of your systems in a sandbox, establishing data consistency (e.g., order and shipping information are consistent between the ordering service and shipping service) is hard when sandboxed systems continually delete their data.

In spite of this, Steve and I believe that a service-oriented approach is the right approach to follow if you want scalability, extensibility, and general goodness.

The Third S: Speed

We have established that service chaining decreases speed and that service-oriented architectures are nice. So why not just have your two services connect at the presentation layer, the top tier of a three-tier architecture, as shown in Figure 9-4?

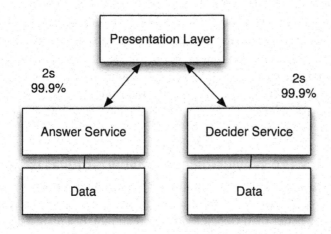

Figure 9-4. Connecting services in the presentation layer

You can do this, but it's not generally a good idea. Asking JavaScript to perform multiple requests is what AJAX is good at, and the worst-case latency in this scenario is two seconds 99.9% of the time. Unfortunately, APIs that are expected in JavaScript tend to be weak in the real world. What's more, you end up with a lot of different dependencies all reflected in a myriad of JavaScript files, and such a system can be difficult to manage.

One way to work around these complexity-management challenges is to load independent parts of your application separately. Put another way, if you have two disjoint features, you can make them completely separate parts of the software, such that the JavaScript files are independent, they can load in parallel, and they can be revised in parallel. The independence of the files and services will help you scale and modify your services quickly. The difference between this approach and the approach where your JavaScript loads everything all at once is *encapsulation*. You want to encapsulate whole functions together so they can work independently.

Caching is another way to solve the service-chaining speed problem. A cache is a copy of a data source. You can have a cache of web pages, a cache of XML, or a cache of a hard disk. You can have a cache of just about anything. Content delivery networks like Akamai are simply caches.

Caches have some interesting and valuable properties that you can exploit to increase your system's speed.

A cache may or may not have a copy of all of the data from its backing store. A system that has all of its data in a cache is considered "cache complete" and has wonderful resiliency properties, because if that backing data store (i.e., a relational database) fails, you can still read your data from the cache.

Cache completeness is nice, but sometimes you want a partial cache. For example, if 90% of your requests are for 10% of your data, you can deploy 100 tiny caches with *only* that 10% of your data, and you'll get performance comparable to having 100 servers 90% of the time. You'll get this performance increase at a tiny fraction of the cost of full servers because caches have very tiny brains. When your service needs something that's not in the cache, it's called a "cache miss"; a good caching scheme will "read through" to the backing store and deliver a value, albeit more slowly than a cache hit will. A bad caching scheme will give you nothing. That's why it's bad.

A smart caching strategy not only reads through to the backing store, but also stores the retrieved value in the cache. This method will either help keep the cache complete or at least keep a count of requests so that the correct 10% of your data lives in the cache. An even simpler approach is to enable the read-through cache to store the value that it retrieved and eject the least recently used cache entry to make space for the new value. Caches designed in this way perform well for content sites like blogs, where new content gets the majority of hits and older content gets less and less traffic over time.

Caches take time to update. When a value in your data store changes, it must be written to the backing store and then the backing store must update all of the caches. In some badly designed environments, this can lead to cache inconsistency, in which a user sees two different values for the same thing. If you can establish stickiness between a user and a cache, then you can implement a write-through cache, in which the value is written first to the cache and then to the backing store.

Caches are either filled up by reading through or by "warming" them. Empty read-through caches produce very bad performance the first time a given value is requested; if you don't want to tolerate this, you need to prefill the cache with your data, which is sometimes called "warming" the cache. You'll have to write additional software to do this.

This is just a cursory explanation of caching, and the good news is that you don't need to know everything about caching to know that it is very important. You now know enough to ask your engineering team intelligent questions about your caching scheme. Or at least you know enough to be suspicious when you find out that you don't have one.

The Fourth S: Scaling

Sometimes caches are not sufficient, however. Sometimes you acquire more users and need your systems to do more than just retrieve additional data—they need to do more thinking. That means you need to provision more servers. One of the great things about third-party hosted services like Amazon's S3 or Google's AppEngine is that they solve many of these problems for you. If you aren't building on these systems, read on.

Before you can scale by adding more servers, you need to understand that your servers look like one server to the user because they'll be behind a *virtual IP*, or VIP. A VIP allows you to present a single Internet address for all the servers you own. VIP addresses are managed by a tricky piece of hardware that allocates each user to a free server and keeps them stuck there. You can buy or lease VIP hardware. They're really, really expensive—you just have to pay. Or, you could follow my previous advice and use a fully hosted stack and avoid this complexity entirely. Now that you can scale by adding more servers, you're going to eventually hear about systems that scale "linearly" or "horizontally." Really geeky dudes may say "constant time" or "N." These all mean the same thing (save for "constant time," which means "I'm smarter than you"): you can add more capacity by adding more servers, and each additional server gives you nearly one full server of additional capacity. In many systems you'll still hit bottlenecks, such as at the VIP—it will only be able to handle so many connections before you have to add a second VIP. One of the nice aspects of service-oriented architectures is that you can scale each service independently, so if the decider service takes more horsepower and the answerer takes more disk space, you can allocate the correct types of hardware and scale them appropriately.

For such a design to work properly, data must be stored so that you can easily spread it across an increasing number of servers. Creating an algorithm to do this can be tricky. Take people's names, for example. You could arrange people's names across 26 servers, one for each letter of the alphabet. This scheme fails because users looking up "Smith" will constantly hammer the S server, and the X, Y, and Z servers will be sitting around wasting space. Luckily, there are less naïve approaches, and you need to make sure that your engineering team is following one of them. One slightly less painful approach is to create a monotonically increasing customer ID for each user and store the data according to customer ID. This allows you to add servers as you add customers.

There are, of course, many ways of storing data on multiple servers so that you scale better. Take your database, for example. Systems that are backed by a single database don't scale horizontally, because they assume that all data exists in a single place, rather than being distributed across multiple servers. Therefore, if you need to scale, you need to buy a bigger server to replace your previous server, which means writing a big check to Oracle and raising your credit limit with Dell. If you have systems like this, you may reach the point where you have more data than you have memory, and results can no longer be cached. Things slow down quickly at this point. Such a system could be said to scale exponentially, or "badly" if it happens to you.

If you're in this pickle, you might want to look at a database technology like NoSQL, which refers to a class of database systems where the data is inherently well distributed across servers. However, because you didn't design the whole storage infrastructure, you can't really define where the data will live or where queries will go. This means that when the data in the database changes, the changes must propagate through the servers, and if you make two queries during this propagation interval you might get inconsistent results. Or, put another way, if you update your system to say I owe you five bucks, you might see that I owe you five bucks and I might see that I owe you nothing. This is not good, but what *is* good is that the results came back quickly and eventually the propagation phase will end. We call this *eventual consistency*. Eventual consistency is probably just fine for things like changes to your résumé, but it's probably not OK for recording bets in a poker game.

You can also work around some kinds of performance bottlenecks by building *indexes*. Indexes help you find the data you need quickly by representing your data in a way that differs from the way it is stored. For example, let's say a user wants to search for "Roger Smith" quickly, but your data is organized on your servers according to customer ID. Without an index, you have to inspect each and every record, which is wildly inefficient. This is referred to as a *table scan*, and if you have these you should start looking to hire a new engineering lead. With an index, you have a list of users sorted by their names, and you can skip right to "Roger Smith" and find his information. Indexes are not free because you must store them and you must update them, but they're worth the cost for common operations.

How to Ask the Right Technical Questions

A few pages on architectures does not a CS degree make. Do not attempt to design a system with only the explanations in this book because you will hurt yourself and others. However, you now know enough to ask your engineering team some important questions and understand most of their answers. The parts you didn't understand were probably *Star Wars* references. You have to ask some of these questions because they will expose potential problems and help your team think through their design. You might believe that your team already thought through the design, considering that they refer to it as a "design." You'd be surprised. Here are some questions you can ask:

Can you please draw me a systems diagram?
>   Your goal is to understand what all the boxes in this systems diagram do. Start with the box closest to the customer and ask what data lives on it, what it does, and what data is sent to and from it. Work your way through all the boxes until you understand what they do. Look for the things we discussed in this chapter, like service isolation, service chaining, indexes, and scaling.

What's the latency for results to be delivered from this box to that box?
>   You should be able to go through the diagram and identify instances of service chaining, question the necessity for that design, and understand what the total response time will be, worst case. If you find a place in the diagram where the latency of a response is really slow, ask how you can improve that by caching, scaling that service horizontally, or separating out some of its logic into other services.

Will this scale for N?
>   Since you're reading this book, it's safe to assume that you'll be wildly successful and therefore the N to which you must scale is a Very Large Number. Ask about what happens when you make this number very large. By "very large," I mean 10,000 requests per second, or 100

million customer records, or 1 million orders per day. What will your engineering team need to do? Can they just add more of box A, or will they need to call Oracle and have the bosses write a painful check?

What happens if I remove box B?

Part of understanding your system is understanding how it will fail and (hopefully) recover. Make sure you understand which parts of the system can create catastrophic failures, and help the engineering team prioritize investments in the stability of those parts.

Are we architected around organizational boundaries or systems boundaries?

Sometimes you'll find that your SOA reflects the way your company is run, rather than the way your data or application is structured. Since your company's organizational structure was not designed to respect Moore's Law, avoid such designs.[1] Some teams have a hard time working together and build redundant or dysfunctional systems; check for this and work against it.

What can we cache to improve performance?

We spent a lot of time on caches because they are important. They increase performance, increase robustness, and decrease operational costs. Identify static data and common lookups and discuss caching them. Don't forget to ask about cache completeness.

What can be loaded independently to improve performance?

Just as we discussed having the answer service and the decider service return results independently, you too should ask if there are parts of the system that can be decoupled. For example, if you can load the advertising separately, such that those systems can function fully independently, you'll have a much more resilient system, and users will be able to complete their primary task even if the advertising system is broken.

---

1   *http://en.wikipedia.org/wiki/Moore%27s_law*

10

How to Be a Great Shipping Communicator

IF YOU ARE TRYING to ship software, you almost certainly have a ton of information to disseminate, statuses to gather, checkups to perform, and other details to sweat. You're going to need to send a lot of email and run a lot of meetings. That's the bad news, but it's why they pay you. The good news is that it's not hard to be great at either one, if you have a little technique.

One key technique is to take as few meetings as possible but no fewer. In many cases, you can avoid the meeting entirely by writing great email. So let's start there, because it's constantly amazing to me how the VPs at Google and Amazon are great at email, while their less experienced team leads are terrible at it. At the very least, you can consider yourself prepared to be a VP at the end of this chapter.

How to Write Great Email

Einstein said, "If you can't say something simply, you don't really understand it." The first thing I do when I get a page-long email to a simple question is archive it, because I've learned that the sender doesn't understand the answer he or she is delivering or has not yet found the right question to ask. The long email syndrome is so pervasive that engineers have developed shorthand for it, replying to these messages: "tl;dr," meaning "too long; didn't read." And if you think anyone can send good email, think again. Kim Rachmeler, the first program manager Amazon hired and former Amazon VP, once singled out a program manager to her team saying, "Her emails were the very embodiment of crispness." This was high praise from one of Amazon's greats. Amazon now requires all people-manager candidates to submit a writing sample as part of the interview process. It's that important.

If the search for praise from your betters or the promise of a generous salary weren't enough, consider that as a great leader you need to constantly deliver clear, specific messages to your team so that they know where they're going and stay aligned with your mission. You must also manage up, which means communicating nuanced details about decisions or progress to people who are even busier and have more email than you do. Writing great email is critical to your success.

Your primary goal in email should be to deliver a single message clearly and succinctly. Within Amazon, people use the word "crisp" a lot to define what a clear and succinct message is. See, Amazon is trying to optimize from two words (clear, succinct) down into one—talk about practicing what you preach! Within Google, however, crisp messages don't play quite so well with individual contributors because the culture is a bit more passive aggressive. More on adjusting to your audience in a moment. You should initially craft email so that it is short, specific, backed up, and delivers a single message clearly. I try to achieve these goals by writing email like a journalist.

WRITE EMAIL LIKE A JOURNALIST

Good journalists start their articles with the most important thing they have to say. A *Wall Street Journal* reporter might write, "The economy still stinks," but you are more likely to start your email with "We're not going to make our date." Follow with the "why" of your statement in the clearest way possible. For example, "because two of our dependencies didn't come in on time." Poorly written email is organized the other way, with excuses and defense up front so the poor reader has no idea for what you're apologizing. For example, the Bad Writer writes:

> It turns out that the name lookup service isn't going to be ready until the 14th. On top of that, two members of our team (Charlie & Sasha) both came down with the flu, so we lost two weeks of productivity. Given these setbacks, which were not our fault, it's unlikely we can make our date.

On the other hand, the Great Writer writes:

> Tom and Jerry,
> We must increase the launch date by two weeks, from 8/7 to 8/21. We
> have to do this because:

- We're behind on development due to illness on the engineering team.
- The Name Lookup Service that we depend on won't be ready until 8/14.

Best,
Chris

In the Bad Writer's email, the writer "buried the lede," which is so common that there's a journalistic nickname for it. A good journalist would never do this without being horribly embarrassed. In the Bad Writer's case, it would be easy for the reader to read that first line and say, "Oh, the date is moved to the 14th." But the date did not move to the 14th; rather, the date is actually two weeks out, since the team lost two weeks.

The Great Writer didn't commit these crimes. The Great Writer also took an additional 20 seconds to add a greeting and a salutation, which helps direct the message to the correct audience (especially when there are people on the cc line), and the salutation may help reduce potential venom. I don't have any evidence that supports my theory about the salutation, but it can't hurt, right? The salutation also saves readers from having to scroll their iPhones back up to the top of the message to figure out who sent it.

Best of all, the Great Writer used the *Great Delta Convention*. I love this writer!

USE THE GREAT DELTA CONVENTION

The Great Delta Convention is a technique you can use to make numbers more easily understandable to people who are reading too quickly. If you want to use the Great Delta Convention, simply format your numbers as follows:

{increase/decrease} Foo by {amount} from {start value} to {end value}

This format lets readers know what's happening—Foo is going to be *increased* or *decreased*. And by how much? The *amount*. But what was it before? You've got that in the *start value*. And if the reader really just cares about what the final ship date is? It's easy to skip ahead to the *end value*. Notice that the Good Writer's update is formatted by the Great Delta Convention:

We must *increase* the launch date *by two weeks*, from *8/7* to *8/21*.

If you want to try for bonus points, make these changes time based by adding the start time, end time, and overall duration to your goal. Your new formula is therefore:

{increase/decrease} Foo by {amount} from {start value} to {end value}
over {period} starting {start time} and ending by {end time}

When you use this format, anyone can quickly see what you're doing, how much impact you're going to have, how long it's going to take, when you're going to start, and when to check back in with you to see if you're done. You accomplished all of these things in just one sentence with no ambiguity. The Great Delta Convention is a powerful tool that can greatly increase clarity. It is also strangely difficult to adopt, so don't feel bad if it seems uncomfortable at first. It's a powerful and simple technique, so it's worth the effort.

PUNCTUATE YOUR EMAIL WITH BULLETS AS REASONS

The Great Writer made this email much easier to scan by visually encapsulating his or her rationale into a single block of bullets. Your team might want to read all the bullets, but if your VP trusts you, she'll skip them and read only the first line of your email. Luckily, you are now a Great Writer, and you wrote a good first line that delivered the most important information first.

If you can't write your rationale as bullets because you don't know the reasons behind your key message, you have a deeper problem. Your best bet is not to send the email, as there's no surer way of looking like an idiot than slipping your date and not knowing why you have to do so. If you must provide an update of some kind, then get out in front of your unfortunate lack of knowledge and don't make guesses. Fall on your sword and promise a date by which you will have the reasons.

By the way: the line spacing of the bullets in the Great Writer's email is meaningful. The proper use of whitespace can help you clearly identify the important, or different, parts of your email.

STOP WRITING NOW, BECAUSE YOU'RE DONE

Your email is done at this point. Maybe you could add a bit more data about your reasons. Maybe you want to add in a link to a dashboard or project plan to show off how really with it you are. You really don't need to do so, because a busy exec can consume this simple email on his or her

BlackBerry and move on. That was your goal, so stop writing now and move on to your next task.

TRY SUGGESTIONS INSTEAD OF QUESTIONS

When you're new on the job, a lot of the email you send will be full of questions, such as: "Why is the Save button red?", "Why have we established a launch date before establishing estimates?", and "Why are we investing in chewing gum?"

These are not actually questions, although the punctuation would have you think so. Rather, they are messages that are heard as "You guys are design idiots," "Do you know anything at all about project management?", and "Chewing gum?!??", respectively. What's worse is that in most places as you start asking these questions, you'll get mixed signals from your team. You'll hear things like, "These are great questions, just ask them differently..." and "People are getting confused by these questions you're asking."

Asking, "Why have we established a launch date before establishing estimates?" is a biased, or leading, question. It asserts the point of view that to establish a launch date before figuring out how much work you have to do is crazy. Of course it is! But for all you know, there might be a contractual deadline or another forcing function driving that date, so at the very least try to prune the bias out of your questions. There's only upside for you if you do.

What's bizarre about this human dynamic around questions is that sometimes (but not always), suggestions are more acceptable than questions. Suggestions allow the other party to be critical of you, whereas questions are directed at the other party and can exacerbate a defensive posture. Perhaps this is evident in the analysis, but it was not obvious to me and it won't be obvious from the feedback you get. So as an experiment, try these Question Suggestions™!

- Can we make the Save button blue?
- Is the launch date negotiable?
- Can I try the chewing gum?

These suggestions might irritate you or me more than the initial set of direct questions, but you'll probably find that they are easier for you to ask a new team.

REMEMBER YOUR AUDIENCE

Sensitivity is painful but necessary in some situations. And when you're a senior leader writing to troops on the front lines, you're going to need to use more of your words. Personally, I care so much about writing crisp email that I frequently deliver blunt decisions and rationale to the individual contributors on the team, and sometimes they don't take it kindly. You know the kind of employee who reacts this way.

I chalk these communication failures up to forgetting my audience. With sensitive groups—such as those who've spent a year working on the product you're about to kill—it's best not to say things like:

> Underling,
> You're fired. This decision was part of our goal to decrease staffing by 10% from 100 to 90 employees. We selected you because:
> - We hate that shirt you wear—you know, the one with the dancing tofu blobs.
> - Your engineering manager didn't stand up for you.
> - Someone had to get the axe.
> Have a nice day,
> Your Boss

Such an email is not likely to be well received, even though it pretty much follows the best practices of which I am so fond. Personally, I wish more people would write these blunt, well-organized email messages, because changing one's wardrobe is much easier than tussling with the existential angst that passive-aggressive email generates. However, you catch more flies with honey...

> Team,
> We have an amazing team of 100 top-notch employees. Over the past year, many of you—a really important 10% of you, in fact—have worked really hard on a system we thought would be really important. Like most things in software, changes happen quickly, and we've recently come to understand that the need for the Wolfgang system has evolved, and we need to pivot the business to better leverage our strengths. This means that we'll stop working on the project today. This change will mean different things to different people, but the gist is that the team working on the Wolfgang project will have to find other opportunities. You should reach out to your engineering manager to discuss this 1:1 as soon as possible.

Please feel free to email me, or your manager, directly if you have any
questions.
Chris

OK, I exaggerate—execs never pay attention to what you wear. But in
general we see this type of email all the time, regardless of company size.
I have a "really" hard time reading this soothing email and figuring out
what it actually says. But many readers prefer the long, sensitive email because it rationalizes the change, compliments folks, and puts the change
in the context of everyone. Also, it uses important buzzwords like "pivot,"
"evolved," "quickly," and so on.

I would like to dismiss this second, sensitive email entirely, but I can't.
Context truly matters. If you're a VP writing for a VP, you *can* send good
email. If you're a line-level product manager or tech lead writing for your
managers, you *must* send good email. If you're a senior manager or VP
writing for your troops, you *must* send sensitive email. If you don't adjust
your email style to your audience, you'll upset a lot of people at both the VP
and the individual contributor levels.

How to Handle the Five Types of Meetings

If your email kung-fu has failed you, it's probably time for a meeting.
Meetings can be painful, or they can be productive and even fun (yes,
you can make meetings fun!). The best way to optimize your meetings
and ensure that they have the potential to be fun is to understand the
structure, purpose, and output of each meeting. There are five types of
meetings you need to hold. They are, in no particular order:

The team meeting
> This meeting collects status and discusses specific issues in depth
> with the goal of resolving those issues as a team. While most of what's
> accomplished in a team meeting could theoretically be resolved over
> email, it never is, so you need this meeting to do that work.

The standup
> The standup is a super-brief meeting that communicates only status
> and provides visibility and accountability for the team. Everyone in the
> meeting stands, which helps keep the meeting brief.

The one-on-one (1:1)

One-on-ones are meetings between you and one other person. These meetings are probably the most rewarding because they enable you to have frank conversations. They also provide a focused time to accomplish collaborative tasks.

The product/engineering/UX review

This is a big meeting, generally with some big bosses, that provides visibility to executives and gathers input from the most experienced people in your organization. Teams carefully prepare for these meetings because they are the most expensive in terms of coping with the inevitable project reset if you do a bad job.

The brainstorming meeting

The most enjoyable of all meetings, the brainstorming meeting is fun because it's free-form, generates ideas, and also enables the team to actively engage in a problem.

THE TEAM MEETING

The team meeting is a 30- to 60-minute weekly meeting with you and your engineering team. You'll likely run it. If you have a tech lead or senior engineer on your team who would be willing to run the meeting, however, by all means, go for it! The goal of this meeting is to keep the team aligned with the mission and reach consensus on currently open issues. Publish an agenda of topics for discussion in advance. Aligning the mission and achieving broad consensus typically become less important as you reach the end of the development process, which means you might be able to cancel the meeting; a good time to think about cancelling the team meeting and moving to relying exclusively on the standup is when you start tracking your bug burndown.

When starting the team meeting, it's always nice to review your metrics. You want to know how the product or development process is going. Were there any outages or significant changes? For example, did Bob spend all week at home with his cat, or did Sally discover a privacy problem that had to be fixed ASAP? Aside from that, how are you doing against your milestones? Generally, this is the point where everyone goes to his or her laptop and updates the columns in the project tracking spreadsheet.

The first time you experience a meeting in which someone walks through a spreadsheet and edits it out loud, you might think, "This is crazy.

We should have done this in advance." You're right—that's the optimal approach, but it's not a realistic approach. Given the ability to do absolutely anything else—like code reviews, writing tests, or reading xkcd.com—an engineer will do that before updating the team spreadsheet. In the team meeting, that same engineer is captive and can do nothing else, and the spreadsheet gets updated. In addition, when talking through the details, the engineer may offer commentary on why some task took more or less time than expected. This commentary is useful to the other team members who may not have known that your build system is twitchy and case-sensitive. For example. Not like that would ever happen in real life.

You can also use the team meeting to check in on higher-level goals. At the beginning of the quarter, I review the team's quarterly goals. We adjust the goals until everyone approves. A mid-quarter check-in helps ensure that the team's status goes from green to yellow to red, rather than going from green to red, which is a good sign that you were asleep at the wheel. At the end of the quarter, we use the team meeting to evaluate our progress against our goals. If you follow this process, your team will stay in control of their future, aligned with project goals, and focused on the right things.

When you're done with the schedule-update part of your meeting, you may want to discuss any developments that the team needs to know about. Important developments may include industry changes, business updates, or other items that are relevant to your mission. Remember, it's your job to keep the team aligned with your mission.

The final part of the team meeting is dedicated to working through open issues. Collect the list of issues that the team needs to discuss at the beginning of the meeting and then work through them one by one after the progress update part of the meeting. Take good notes, assign action items, and follow up. After you've finished dealing with these issues, ask the team if there is anything else they want to discuss. Wait seven seconds for an answer. Seven seconds feels like a very long time to wait, but that slightly uncomfortable silence is just enough to ensure that the most introverted person on your team speaks up.

Generally, I find that even a short team meeting is better than none, since it gives the whole team an opportunity to get together in a different way, and it can also serve as a break. I try to hold a brief meeting to check in with the team even if I don't think there is anything to discuss. I am frequently surprised by what I discover during the quiet seven seconds I spend staring at various teammates!

THE STANDUP MEETING

Scrum and agile development advocates swear by the daily standup. The best standups actually have everyone stand. The thinking behind a true "standing" meeting is that it gets folks away from their computers and on their feet, where they are less comfortable, so the meetings are forced to be shorter. I like to use these meetings on a daily basis because they drive accountability and transparency across the team. Each person should report the following:

- What I did yesterday
- What I'm doing today
- If I am blocked

If you do this, the entire team will have visibility into individual performance and the status of the project. Blocking issues will emerge quickly. Best yet, challenges are frequently met with offers of help. For example, when Jenny says, "I've been fighting with this build, I can't get test X to pass," it's not uncommon to see her fellow engineer Sean say, "Yep, that happened to me last week. Let's talk after the meeting; maybe I can help." This kind of visibility saves a lot of time in the long run.

My teams at Google and Amazon liked to hold standup meetings for less than 15 minutes at 11:30 or 12 p.m. These times occur just before lunch, so the team was already at a breaking point and probably not in a state of "flow." It's also critical to have someone, like the program manager or development lead, watch out for discussions that become too detailed. For example, if Sean and Jenny end up in a conversation about why test X isn't passing, someone needs to say, "Hey, can you guys take that offline?" This approach enables the standup to keep going and stay short.

You can get in and get out of a 10-person standup meeting in less than 10 minutes. I've seen 50-person standup meetings at Google take less than 20 minutes, but they were mainly useful for reiterating goals, not collecting status.

I'm not an advocate of the Scrum Chicken approach, which says that only developers should speak. I'm a fan of transparency, and I love having product management, engineering management, design, user experience researchers, and even interns contribute to the standup when they can. My engineering teams love to hear the 30-second snippet of what's going on with business development, because it helps reinforce that the project is bigger than just them.

I also like having the development lead provide a 30-second brief on the status of the project. It's a nice way to set the context of the meeting and remind the team of critical things. Here's an example of a development lead update you can copy:

> Today we have 30 bugs, our find/fix ratio is finally going down, and we're still planning on a dogfood release by the end of next week, so get your changes in by Tuesday, end of day. Remember, Tuesday, EOD. And I'm on call, so my productivity will probably be down this week.

THE 1:1 MEETING

One-on-ones are incredibly useful meetings for leads to have together because they allow for frank conversations and expose new issues. They are also a great forum for getting work done because they are small and focused. You can easily take two minutes in your 1:1 to send the email that you and your coworker agreed to send, rather than taking an action item to do it after the meeting. This approach saves you time you would otherwise spend context switching and reduces the chance that a task won't get done. Similarly, you and your marketing lead might take the last 15 minutes of your 30-minute 1:1 to rework the first paragraph of your blog post collaboratively. Doing work during meetings is one of the best uses of them.

Schedule weekly or biweekly 1:1s with all your leads, even if you don't think you'll need them. The duration of your 1:1 will be a function of how much you need to cover or do; 30 minutes is a good starting point, but a 50-minute 1:1 is not out of the question. You might discover things in these meetings that you didn't know you needed to discuss. If the meeting is not productive after a few weeks, you can cancel it or reschedule it so it occurs once per month.

THE PRODUCT, UX, AND ENGINEERING DESIGN REVIEWS

"Reviews" of any kind are generally big meetings with the big bosses. The goal of the first of these reviews, the product review, is to get leaders bought into your product direction, solicit feedback, or update your leadership on your status. All of the suggestions from the "How to Build and Give a Great Presentation" section later in this chapter apply to the review. Figure out what your precise message is and then deliver it as clearly and concisely as you can. Because the audience for these meetings tends to be very busy, it's best to keep reviews short—30 minutes or less.

The only materials you need for a UX review are your mocks. It's best for designers to present their own mocks. If your designer is going to present, take a moment at the beginning of the meeting and set the stage by reminding everyone why you're there, who the user is, and what your business goal is. You'll want to run the presentation only if your designer is a down-in-the-weeds type of person and past experience has taught you that you'll be more successful presenting a higher-level walkthrough.

The goal of an engineering review is to empower your development lead, collect technical feedback from the most experienced engineers around, and spend as little time as possible on the presentation. Review the materials in advance to ensure that the development team isn't proposing something outside your mission or divergent with your strategy. If you've done a good job communicating these two things to your team, you won't have problems. If you're not the engineering lead who's presenting, then your goal in the engineering review is to handle curveballs from senior management when they ask, "Wait, why are we building feature X?" It's always best to have the engineering lead answer questions like this, because answering these questions will empower him or her, which was one of your goals. You'll frequently find such questions catch your engineering lead flat-footed. When this happens, chime in. The last message you want delivered is the one that says your team doesn't know what's going on.

THE BRAINSTORMING MEETING

The final and most fun type of meeting is the brainstorming meeting. The goal of a brainstorming meeting is to collect as many ideas as possible, regardless of whether the ideas are names for your product, solutions to your scaling problem, or possible root causes for a system failure. Brainstorming meetings can be any length at all, but do your best to take a break after an hour and a half!

Brainstorming meetings can be fun free-for-alls, but if you want them to work well you have to establish some ground rules. I have four ground rules that I follow, and I'm confident that they increase the creative output of the brainstorming meeting. The rules are:

- Don't criticize when you're brainstorming.
- Say, "Yes, and..."
- Prompt discussion with structure.
- Be clear when the brainstorming is over.

Don't criticize when you're brainstorming

The surest way to stomp on creative ideas is to critique them. Critique is a fancy way of saying "criticize." All it takes is one Negative Nellie in the conference room, and you'll lose one of your valuable idea-generating teammates. Start your meeting by articulating this rule. One way you can help avoid criticism and encourage people to volunteer ideas is by writing everything on the whiteboard. Those giant, easel-sized Post-it notes work great too. Big Post-its are nice because you can take them with you when you're done.

Say, "Yes, and..."

There's a rule in improvisational theater that actors developed (or perhaps evolved, in the face of lots of booing) to prevent scenes from stalling. It's the "Yes, and..." rule, which says that regardless of whatever your acting partner says, you respond with "Yes, and..." Even if your partner says, "Oh, now your pants are on fire!" you have to respond, "Yes, and...it's because I farted into my lighter! *Why* do I keep that in my back pocket?!?"

You might be surprised how well this trick works in a business context. It takes ideas to the next level. Encourage your teams to use it.

Prompt discussion with structure

W. Edwards Deming is a legend in the business community because of the innovative processes he brought to industry. Old stodgy guy that he was, he still believed in brainstorming. He used fishbone diagrams (more about those in a bit) to record and direct these meetings. Each spine in the diagram was a question he would pose and then his teams would brainstorm possible answers to that question. When they ran out of ideas, they would brainstorm possible causes for each answer that was just brainstormed, and so on, until they reached the root cause of the problem. Or got bored.

Adding structure can encourage and organize creativity. You need not use fishbone diagrams. Sometimes even setting an agenda of three problems to solve and working through them can help the more technical, highly organized members of your team engage in your process.

Be clear when the brainstorming is over

It's fun to brainstorm, but you can't do it all day long. At some point, you'll have to end the brainstorming and go through a critical analysis phase. It's important to articulate to the team that you're switching modes, because if you don't, you might bounce back randomly into pure creative mode, and some people with new ideas might feel rejected when you try to put the meeting back on track.

Edward De Bono wrote about changing your thinking mode in his book *Six Thinking Hats* (Back Bay Books). He argued that we should take off the "green" creative hat and put on the "black" critical hat to analyze these options. The hats are his way of saying that you need to make a strong transition from one way of thinking to the other way of thinking, and be explicit about the transition. There are four other hats he describes if you'd like to expand your mental wardrobe further.

How to Run a Good Meeting

Every leader will run his or her meetings somewhat differently. Meetings are frequently a manifestation of your personal style, which means that there's no best way to run all meetings. However, there are some best practices that can make every meeting you run better, regardless of your personal style or the type of meeting you're holding. In addition to the advice in Chapter 11 on how to deal with conflict, which applies to conflict in meetings, the four best practices I follow are:

- Send headline notes immediately.
- Allow your meeting's objective to change.
- Stamp out negativity in team meetings; embrace it in 1:1s.
- Use tools like fishbone diagrams to facilitate problem solving.

SEND HEADLINE NOTES IMMEDIATELY

Peter Drucker was an executive performance guru and author of *The Effective Executive* (HarperBusiness). He was a proponent of sending notes to everyone concerned after a meeting. Jonathan Rosenberg, former SVP of all product managers at Google, was such an ardent advocate of sending meeting notes that he asked to be cc'd, personally, on all meeting notes from meetings with more than five attendees. None of the product managers working for him was ever able to figure out how he handled the volume of email he received.

You'll want to send notes immediately after your meeting ends in order to maximize the impact they have and so that your team will feel included. Don't worry excessively about the accuracy of your notes; if you make a mistake, people will correct you. Lead your notes with the conclusions and next steps. Include the nitty-gritty details later in the notes so that readers who disagree with the conclusions can understand why the team reached them. This note-taking technique should be self-evident, but at Google I saw notes from PMs all the time that were unreadable because they contained only details. Write a crisp, two- to five-line summary, stick it at the top of your notes, and people will thank you. It's nice to be thanked, don't you think?

ALLOW YOUR MEETING'S OBJECTIVE TO CHANGE

Meetings exist to serve one or more of three key purposes: to solve a problem, to collect information, or to disseminate information. A weekly team meeting can sometimes accomplish all three things, if you are able to help it evolve.

The most important thing to remember when running a large review-scale meeting is that even though your goal was to disseminate information ("This is our plan..." you'll say), you may have to pivot quickly and start collecting information. This might happen if one of your underlying assumptions changed. Follow the advice later in this chapter in the section "How to Build and Give a Great Presentation," which talks about how to pivot, listen carefully, and collect this information.

When you're in a team meeting and you discover a problem—whether it's team dynamics or a systems design problem or a new requirement—embrace it. Remember from Chapter 5 that "bad news is good news." Embrace the bad news head-on and address it. I believe you should put the bad news in your meeting notes right away. You can add that "the team is investigating this issue actively," if you want to reassure execs who are prone to panic. Most are, of course.

In a meeting where bad news emerges, you'll need to play a facilitation role. You must first recognize that your information dissemination meeting is now focused on problem solving; help the team pivot to that objective by stating that the meeting's focus has changed. You might say, "Let's pause for a moment and try to solve this, OK?" Alternatively, you can acknowledge the problem, identify an owner and next steps, and take the issue offline to be resolved in the right context. Your team will tell you which approach they prefer, and since you are a servant of your team, follow their guidance. For the most part. Some teams will avoid conflict at all costs, and you'll need to create a safe space for them to work it out; that's facilitation.

STAMP OUT NEGATIVITY IN TEAM MEETINGS; EMBRACE IT IN 1:1S

I firmly believe that nearly all crises are teaching opportunities. One such opportunity is when members of your team start to whine. Unlike team meetings, 1:1 meetings are a great place for individuals to vent. In this smaller arena, you can be a sounding board and help your teammates process their feelings by using basic active listening techniques, such as saying, "I hear you saying X." But when one person in a team meeting is being strongly negative and dismissing people or the product, you need to stomp on that attitude. Persistent negativity is poison to a team, so use the crisis to teach the team how to respond constructively, instead of whining. One example of how you can do this is by pointing out where the whiner has the power to make changes. You can also reiterate your mission and identify what's going well. I don't advocate arguing the specific point that your teammate raises. Rather, offer to meet 1:1 with him or her to work through the specific issue, rather than arguing in front of the team.

USE TOOLS LIKE FISHBONE DIAGRAMS TO SOLVE PROBLEMS

In team meetings, where you're trying to solve a problem, one of the most effective things you can do is ask the "Five Whys." This is an approach embraced by Deming that suggests you should keep asking "why?" until you get to the root cause, which will generally take you five tries. Some teams start by brainstorming and trying to throw out general solutions, but I don't find that this is the most effective approach, and neither did Deming. He liked to use fishbone diagrams as a way of building out answers to the Five Whys.

For example, let's pretend you have a problem with sales; your sales problem is the spine of your fish (see Figure 10-1).

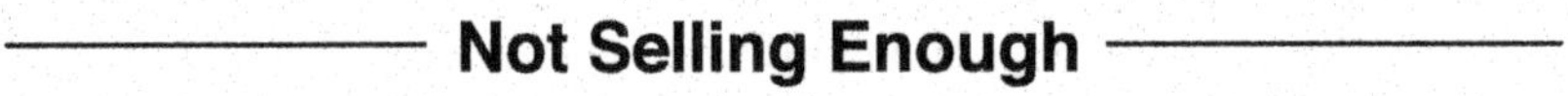

——————————— **Not Selling Enough** ———————————

Figure 10-1. Spine of the fishbone diagram

Next, the team should brainstorm answers to the question "Why aren't we selling enough?" Instead of writing your team's ideas on the whiteboard as a list, put each idea on a line extending from the spine, as shown in Figure 10-2.

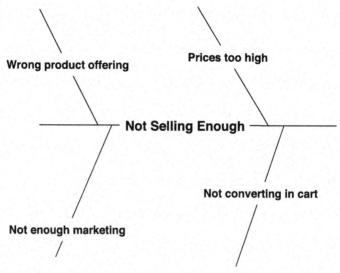

Figure 10-2. Fishbone diagram—the first why

When you've added this first layer of bones, go through each bone and ask "why?" The product guru on your team should know that marketing hasn't changed and neither have your prices or product selection. Now it's time to ask why users aren't converting in the cart. Add the answers to this question to their respective bones (Figure 10-3).

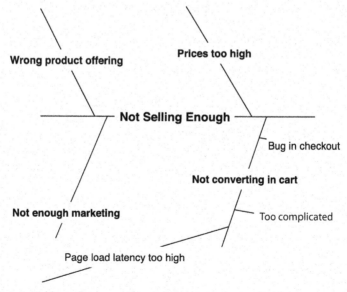

Figure 10-3. Fishbone diagram—the second why

With your team, you've brainstormed some reasons. You know that you haven't changed the process, but there could be a bug. Your test team agrees to run a test pass against production. But you've also noticed that page load latency is much higher than it should be—five seconds 99% of the time! Why is page latency too high? (See Figure 10-4.)

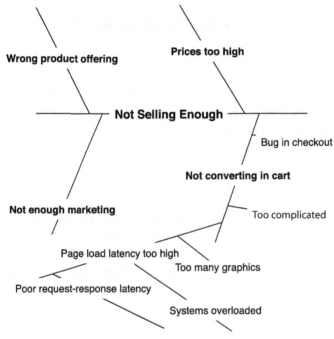

Figure 10-4. Fishbone diagram—the third why

Let's apply data to this example. Your systems are running at 30% CPU, and your designer comments that your graphics are minimal and sprited (these are answers to the possible causes in Figure 10-4). So the cause must have something to do with request-response latency, which is actually 4.5 seconds 99% of the time! Why is latency so high? (See Figure 10-5.)

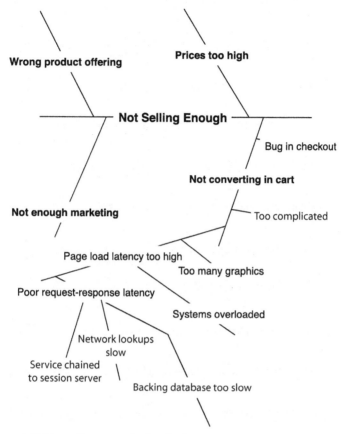

Figure 10-5. Fishbone diagram—the fourth why

This is getting interesting, and the diagram is getting complicated, but we aren't at root cause yet. Based on the information in Chapter 9, we should ask someone to look into the service-chaining problem, but the session server isn't causing anyone else problems. We're left with the backing database, which is slower than we expect. Why? (See Figure 10-6.)

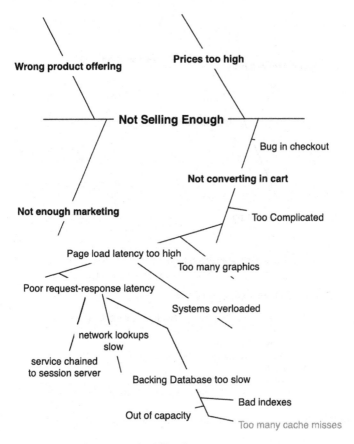

Figure 10-6. Fishbone diagram—the fifth why

Aha! Let's pretend that your team doesn't have enough expertise to understand why the backing database is too slow. A reasonable next step would be to take that investigation offline and consult a database architect (DBA). This DBA looks at the database, and it turns out you have a very high rate of cache misses, causing lots of disk reads (see the section "The Third S: Speed," in Chapter 9, for more on caching). This is your root cause. Luckily, when your DBA adjusts the amount of memory allocated to the cache, sales increase by 10% and you are duly promoted. Nice work!

Even if you don't use a specific fishbone diagram, you can still use the Five Whys technique. First write down each potential problem, then drill into the problems, and finally write down the discussion in your notes. This process will help your team understand that they've thought through the problem well, and you'll also feel confident that you solved the right problem. You may need to spend multiple meetings or weeks working through this process, but that's OK as long as you reach a root cause.

Throughout this discussion, it is important to understand what your role is. We arrived at a pretty technical answer to this problem. Your role during this conversation, however, was not to find the problem, but rather to facilitate the discussion. You kept asking "why?" You went to experts who knew things you might not know, like your engineering team, your designer, and eventually a DBA. You didn't have the answers at the start of the investigation, but you kept asking why. Good work—that's how you'll ship a great product.

How to Build and Give a Great Presentation

If you are trying to ship great software, you will deliver a lot of presentations. For example, you may deliver a presentation to get funding. You may build decks to provide product updates. You might even pitch to convince people to work with your team. Clearly, building great decks and delivering a great presentation is a critical skill, but it is one that can take years to master. Steve Jobs–level presentations are the gold standard, but they are incredibly time-consuming to build, probably have more compelling content than you do, and are generally beyond the reach of most of us.

The good news is, if you spend a lot of time going to presentation classes, studying speaking, getting coaching, and so on, you'll find that there are some basic things you can do to help ensure that your presentation is great, and then you can continue the business of shipping. The great news is, I've written down the basic rules and techniques. The bad news? You still have to do the presentation. Here are the tips in a nutshell:

- Limit your presentation to 15 minutes.
- Always have one, and only one, message.
- Tell a story.
- Build the "deck in one slide."
- Lead with the user experience.
- Listen like crazy.

LIMIT YOUR PRESENTATION TO 15 MINUTES

Your goal should be to deliver a 10- to 15-minute presentation. Many leaders routinely break the rule of maximum presentation length because they are so deep into the details, have so much data to share, and believe that the problem they are addressing is very complicated. These are valid reasons, but they ignore the reality of the situation. The reality is that you typically have only 30 minutes in which you must deliver your message, discuss it to ensure comprehension, and get approval. Even if you are lucky enough to be scheduled for an hour or longer, it's important to remember that 15 minutes of content is all that a typically overworked group of executives can handle in one sitting.

The 15-minute presentation in a 30-minute period typically follows this timeline:

00:00 – 00:05 *(5 minutes)*

Waiting. Every meeting seems to start five minutes late.

00:05 – 00:15 *(10 minutes)*

Deliver your presentation.

00:15 – 00:25 *(10 minutes)*

Discussion and questions about your presentation. If this happens during your presentation, that's OK; some presentations will take longer but generate fewer questions. Remember that you have a total of 20 minutes to cover both the presentation and the questions.

00:25 – 00:30 *(5 minutes)*

Restate the conclusions and key feedback, and agree on the next steps. If you listened very carefully, you might be able to restate the conclusions and key feedback in less than five minutes, in which case you'll be done early and your audience will treat you to admiring nods.

It should be clear from this timeline that you need to aim to create a presentation that is shorter than 10 minutes, and force the length of your presentation to less than 15 minutes. If you work at a company where your meetings always start and end on time, maybe you can stretch your presentation by five minutes, but I'd encourage you not to push it. You never know when a key stakeholder will get caught in the hall or have to take a call from daycare. It's best to assume that you lose at least five minutes in every meeting. It may seem impossible to compress your content into five minutes, but you can do it if you have only one message and you stay on it, which brings us to the next tip.

ALWAYS HAVE ONE, AND ONLY ONE, MESSAGE

Whether your message is "We have a killer idea that needs funding," "We must make a decision to target consumers or businesses," or "We're on track with 90% probability of making our date," you need to have a key message. Cancel the presentation if you don't know what your message is.

You may believe that you have two messages that are critical to deliver. You'll be served best if you deliver only one message and schedule a second meeting. There are three good reasons why you should deliver only one message per meeting:

- First, trying to deliver two messages runs the risk of conflating the two messages. Your audience is probably very bright, but they came from a very different meeting just before yours, and are going into a different meeting after your meeting, so they will have a difficult time switching context an additional time. If you make life easy on your audience, they will love you.
- Second, you will have two ideas competing for primary importance in the discussion. You will implicitly ask your audience to prioritize the topics you brought to the meeting, and you want them to focus on your content—not on prioritizing it. Managing two messages will also make the meeting harder for you to guide.
- Third, and perhaps most important, you forced your presentation to be less than 15 minutes, and because you're a great presenter you culled the presentation down to 10 minutes. The probability that you can deliver two messages in 10 minutes is between 0 and –1. You simply won't have the time to deliver two messages.

Once you have your one message prepared, stay on message. Eliminate data or topics that don't speak to your message. If it helps you feel better, put supporting items like charts and customer quotes into an appendix. You can then jump to the eliminated topic if it comes up in the discussion. Each slide title should build on the message. For example, if you're giving your status report presentation, and your message is "We're on track," the title for your bug burndown slide might be "Find/fix trending at 2/5." You can complete that sentence by adding, "which proves that..." and your message. Ergo, "Find/fix trending at 2/5—we're on track." If each slide in your presentation stays on message, you'll ensure that your message is delivered, even if the audience is checking their email.

Don't forget to double-check your deck after you're done with it to ensure that it's still on message; frequently you'll find that you recast your message as a result of the thinking that went into the presentation. That's great; that kind of thinking is precisely what's supposed to happen during the development phase of your deck, but go back through it and ensure that it remains focused on one, and only one, message.

TELL A STORY

Humans love stories. Stories are engaging and connect messages to our real lives. You'll be much more effective if you try to tell a story with your presentation wherever you are presenting to humans.

Let's prove this tip with an example. Say you have a killer idea that needs funding. In your pitch, you could be like most of us and start with the details of your idea, like:

> By recontexualizing social sharing into a mobile environment, using autogenerated metadata and UGC, we've created an application that will radically increase participation and virally grow adoption.

Yup, that's a terrible, horrible, no good, very bad pitch. It has acronyms and buzzwords, and is unclear. What if you used twice as many words and pitched it through a story?

> Imagine you're at a restaurant and not only have you just had the best lobster of your life, but it's also the first lobster your wife ever had. It's an amazing experience, and by the time you get home to type all this into Facebook, you're exhausted, you won't bother, and you won't capture it well. What if you could, with one button push on your smartphone, share this experience? We can do that—and with that one button click, we'll attach the name of the restaurant, your name, your wife's name, and a picture.

I bet you can see the slide right now. You would show a picture of your happy wife eating lobster and tell the story over it. You might even be able to expense your lobster dinner. You've created a story worthy of Steve Jobs, and you told it in less time than your audience would take processing the first sentence of the original pitch.

In addition to eliminating buzzwords and acronyms, you accomplished five other things with this story:

- **You made it personal and engaged with your audience.** Dining at a restaurant is something most of us can understand.
- **You asked the audience to come with you.** By saying "Imagine..." and "What if?", you invited the audience to respond by making an implicit commitment to listen for a short time. And you've piqued their interest!
- **You provided a concrete example that we can understand.** New ideas are complicated, and audiences need a frame of reference so they can catch up to where you are. In your case, being out at dinner and wanting to share with a smartphone is something we understand. In the film industry, people say things like "It's like *Die Hard* meets *Forrest Gump* meets *Hackers*, but with heart," because these concrete examples give busy executives a shortcut to understand the new concept.
- **You described the problem you will solve.** And you captured it clearly.
- **You described how the solution improves the life of the user.** From the beginning of Chapter 1, you'll remember that both Larry Page at Google and Jeff Bezos at Amazon believe adamantly in putting the user first. You need to communicate how you're going to improve the life of a user in your story, and you did it in this one.

I frequently see technically biased presenters dive into features rather than describing user scenarios. Effective executives frequently stop presenters who do this in the middle of their presentation and force the presenter to articulate a scenario by saying something like "Hold on—I need an example. Let's take my sister Sharon. She uses a smartphone and we're out at dinner. What happens next?" By the time this happens, you're already in a risky place because you must work within the executive's story framework, which is hard to do on your feet. You're much better off starting with a story.

Unfortunately, some presentations don't lend themselves well to stories. Saying something like "Let me tell you a story of a bold team. A noble team. A team that needs to slip their date..." is a bad idea, so let's not go that far. In a status update, you simply have to deliver evidence that backs up your message. Other presentations, such as user experience reviews or pitches, lend themselves to stories because you can organize your content around the user.

BUILD THE "DECK IN ONE SLIDE"

Peter Wilson, a former Google engineering director, invented the "deck in one slide" approach. Peter might not be the Steve Jobs speaker type (who is?), but he was incredibly effective at delivering a message and cutting to the chase with overly distracted executives. That he sold his startup to Facebook as a "talent acquisition" should speak to his ability to spin a yarn!

Peter's "deck in one slide" approach says that the first slide of your presentation, after the title slide, must contain the essence of your presentation. Use this slide when you have skeptical management who are likely to jump to conclusions. By distilling your entire presentation down into one slide, you can short-circuit preconceived notions they have.

Another benefit of the "deck in one slide" is that it gives you a visual element to dwell on if (or when) your presentation goes awry. It's not uncommon for investors or executives to obsess about something you think is irrelevant. It's not just you, it happens to all of us from time to time. If you have built this special slide, you can flip to it and use it to steer the conversation back on track.

Unfortunately, the "deck in one slide" approach doesn't play well with the "tell a story" technique, so use it carefully and particularly when you have execs who want to jump ahead.

The "deck in one slide" should have the following four items:

What you're there to discuss
> Avoid acronyms or new names. You will almost certainly want to use acronyms in order to save space. Don't—your audience may or may not know the acronym, and you should err on the side of not requiring your audience to think. Code names are also likely to distract and confuse your audience since your management or investors are unlikely to have heard your latest code name. The less you have to teach your executives, the better. A nice crisp example of a great first bullet is "The checkout experience is broken."

The opportunity
> Put another way, why are you and the execs spending time discussing this topic? For example, "80% of users abandon the purchase process, representing an opportunity cost of $10M." Note that I put my two essential data points in here. You can probably distill the core data in your presentation down into one or two important data points. Adding these points to your "deck in one slide" adds legitimacy to it and addresses doubt out of the gate. If a major hiring criteria for team leads

is "must be quantitative" (see Chapter 8), using numbers in this slide will help reassure your bosses that they made a good hiring decision.

The proposed solution

To continue our previous example, you'll want to be concrete, but it's hard to use pictures in the "deck in one slide." State your solution crisply: "Add no-login purchasing. Reduce the buy steps from 5 to 2." Provide a link to the mocks so you can pull them up quickly if you need to.

The cost and timeframe to implement

In some cases, this might also be the "Ask" bullet, because it's what you want your management to give you. It might be "2 engineers for 2 months," or "Approval to launch." You can't stop there, however. If your management is going to commit to you, they expect a similar commitment to them. You need to provide a timeline to which you can be held accountable. For example, you might write "Dogfood in February, ship in March."

Figure 10-7 shows what the completed "deck in one slide" looks like. It lacks visual design (intentionally—I don't want people to think I wear a suit to work!), and you can see how easy it is to understand what we're going to talk about, what we need, and when we're going to deliver if the presentation goes well. Which it will.

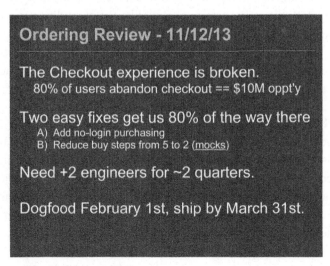

Figure 10-7. The "deck in one slide"

Once you've written this slide, you can build the remainder of the deck, which will be about four slides plus one conclusion slide that focuses on your tasks. A five-slide deck is all you can comfortably fit into a 15-minute presentation.

LEAD WITH THE USER EXPERIENCE

One of the best ways to break past preconceived assumptions and create a concrete picture is to use pictures. Specifically, lead with mockups of the user experience. Start with the user and move through screenshots. In the slide following our "deck in one slide" shown in Figure 10-7, we'd likely show screenshots of how awful the current five-step checkout pipeline is. These images would help cement the problem in the minds of the audience. Also, when you show the audience the beautiful no-login purchasing process, they'll be ecstatic at the contrast.

You will still need to state the message when you lead with the UX. It's a good idea to use the "deck in one slide" approach to state the message and set the context of the meeting. Alternatively, you can be very simple and just state it on the title slide, like: "Product Review for: Approval of the iPhone App User Experience." As you're waiting for the meeting to start, the audience will see the title and clearly understand what they will be asked to do. In this example, it's product review and they need to approve the iPhone app user experience.

To work from the user outward in your mocks, state the primary user goal, rather than describing features. You can then point to how the user experience addresses the goal. If you've done a great job designing your product's UX, the primary user goal will be the most discoverable, simplest part of the UI. You can move to the next slide just as a user would tap or click through the UI. This approach enables the audience to continue thinking through the visuals as if they are users. This technique helps build a strong narrative.

LISTEN LIKE CRAZY

If you've followed the plan so far, you have only one more essential thing to do: listen. It's incredibly hard to listen and present at the same time, but it's imperative that you do so. Your ability to pick up on nuanced objections and understand which ones are deal breakers and which ones are just complaints is critical. The difference between suggestions and requirements is the difference between shipping greatness and not shipping at all.

One technique that works well for capturing nuanced comments is to bring a trusted associate who will take verbatim notes. By capturing the exact words that were said, you allow much less room for subjective debate. You'll still debate what the words mean, but not what was said.

If you don't have someone to take verbatim notes, bring a pad with you and write down the feedback from the essential stakeholders. Understanding who the key stakeholders are in advance will enable you to focus on the right feedback and use your note-taking time efficiently. For example, when presenting at Google, I knew to always pay attention to what Eric, Larry, and Sergey said (in that order), but take the guidance from other members of the executive group as good advice. Frequently the best advice would come from these other members, but they were not going to block the product launch, so their input was less critical regardless of how good it was. The same approach was true for Jeff Bezos and his senior management team (a.k.a. the "S-Team"); it was critical to write down what Jeff said word-for-word and take the management team's guidance as good advice.

At the end of the presentation, it's vital that you clarify any statements from key stakeholders that you don't understand. If Jeff said, "It might be a good idea..." then you probably want to revisit that topic. "Jeff, just to close on this—do you think we should delay the launch to do X?" Do this sparingly and only when you must. Don't oversell. I once had Eric Schmidt stop me, saying, "You can stop talking; you're approved. Let's move on." If you can get in and out in half the time you had planned for your meeting, great!

BONUS PRESENTATION TIPS

- If you can't have one picture and one sentence per slide, put the main message in the title. The Apple crew is genius at this, but it's really best for pitching to people outside or bigger groups.
- If you can't follow the preceding tip, put the main message in the title.
- If you have no template, use basic, business-school blue background with yellow and white fonts. They show up great on any projector.
- Read and follow the basic visual design principles in *The Non-Designer's Design Book* by Robin Williams (Peachpit Press).
- Read and follow the information presentation principles in Edward Tufte's book *The Visual Display of Quantitative Information*, Second Edition (Graphics Press).

- Don't be afraid of whitespace. Sparse slides are good.
- Don't use builds, unless you want your audience to think you wear a suit.
- Don't use the color red to mean anything other than danger or bad.

11

How to Make Great Decisions

THE THING THAT'S DIFFERENT between software and English is not the language. C++ and Dickens share many of the same words. What's different is that software is the physical embodiment of decisions. Because you can do anything in software (don't let anyone tell you otherwise), the decisions your team makes about what your software will do, and how it will do it, are skeletons of your product.

Unfortunately, making decisions is not as simple as you saying "yes" or "no" to your team. Unlike most other compilations of English words, the complexity of software mandates that it is the creation of a group, and therefore it is a reflection of the decisions that the group makes. In some cases a Big Boss can dictate decisions. Unluckily, you are not the Big Boss, and you must enable your team to find ways to say no to the things they love. Here's how to get the job done. If it bears any similarity to convincing a small child to go to bed instead of finishing watching *Thomas & Friends*, I'm sorry.

You will start by trying to defer the request. "We'll finish it tomorrow," you'll say to little Johnny, who is the world's biggest Thomas the Tank Engine fan. If Johnny starts to cry terribly, and you're a sucker, you'll try the next technique, which is negotiating. "OK, OK, sssssshhhh...10 more minutes, OK? 10?" The negotiation process can be complicated—certainly Johnny will argue for 15—but if you study this chapter, you'll probably reach a good middle ground with both you and Johnny happy about Thomas. Of course, there's always a risk that Johnny is simply overtired and confrontational. When this happens, you need to bring all of your conflict management skills to bear, like understanding that most conflict is the result of miscommunication, understanding what triggered Johnny's response, and using personas to depersonalize conversations. I doubt personas will help you with Johnny, but they will help you depersonalize conflict in your business negotiations. Let's look at each of these approaches in more detail.

Postponing: "We'll Finish It Tomorrow"

"Featuritis" is a common affliction because we humans are afraid of conflict, and many software team leads are afraid to say no. Sometimes the fear isn't of conflict, but rather of not being good enough; software team leads are frequently afraid that the software won't do everything it could and acutely aware of how much it could do. This attitude leads to fear-based design and in turn generates overly complicated products that never ship. There's a simple solution to this problem.

Any feature that isn't part of the absolute minimum viable feature set can go into V2. The test for any feature is, "Can the user complete the basic task for which this software was invented?" If the user can complete the task without the feature, even if the accomplishment of that task was particularly painful and ugly, then the feature can go into V2. You must be diligent about this test, because every line of code (except for unit tests!) decreases the probability of shipping, and without shipping there is no greatness.

If you suggest that a feature go into V2 and you hit resistance, it's time to negotiate.

Negotiation: "OK, 10 More Minutes"

Nearly every feature or user experience debate ends up as some form of hostage negotiation. You have their baby, or they have yours, and unless someone's way is gotten...the baby gets it. Whether you're debating if a bug is a blocker or the icons should be green or blue, this conversation is a negotiation—and the baby in jeopardy is your product. If you were the Big Boss, you could take the baby and run, but you're not. Instead, you probably have little or no legitimate authority, so negotiating to a great consensus quickly is critical to your success.

The first step in negotiating properly is to understand that even though you are a product owner, you're not the boss. Your team is working with you because they like you or they like the product. They're not working on your product because they have to. It's a given in the software industry that anyone you'd want to work with could easily work somewhere else. Therefore, it's critical to bring your team along in the decision-making process and enable them to own the product with you.

Team leads commonly make the mistake of conducting decision-making meetings in small groups. Having a small meeting seems efficient on its face, but isolating the meeting from your engineering team can isolate the team from the decision-making process. If you isolate the team from decisions, they will disengage from the product development process and leave you. If you want to be great at shipping, you need a team that feels engaged and empowered to participate and voice their concerns.

A better process for team decision making is to engage with all the members of the team at an early stage, before your plans are finalized. In my experience, this approach is more efficient in the long term because you have the opportunity to explain the business objectives and team goals to the entire team at the beginning of the project. If you instead have many small meetings with senior stakeholders and then deliver a fully baked plan, you will probably need many more small meetings to deal with concerns that arise late in the game. Even worse, one or more of those concerns might be legitimate and cause some substantial change in your plans. Good project management technique says that you want to take all changes as early as possible in the development process.

Management guru Peter Drucker has a slightly different take in his book *The Effective Executive*, arguing that you want to have brief meetings with clear goals and relatively few attendees. His advice differs a bit from mine, but he also says that the effective executive should publish the agenda for the meeting to all concerned parties and plan to send clear notes afterward. This enables concerned parties to join the meeting and marginally concerned parties to understand the outcome. The details in his approach align well with what I suggest, so feel free to follow Peter's advice, even though it is somewhat less collaborative.

If there's a guiding principle that you should embrace when thinking about whom to involve in decisions, it's transparency. Be transparent about *why* decisions are made. Be transparent about *when* decisions will be made. Be transparent about *how* your team can engage in the product process.

Once you've brought the right people together, you need to negotiate to consensus, not to a victory for yourself. Many software leaders can be a bit macho, and this leads to a victory-first approach. In a classic example, a young, tough, macho Google product manager went into a naming review at Google to decide the public name for his product. He was remembered by the marketing team later as saying, "Let's call it Google Turbo!" and was, unfortunately, laughed at. Macho tends to be bossy, confrontational, and occasionally comic.

It is therefore unsurprising to me that many of the best software leads are women, even though men primarily populate the profession. Anita Woolley and Thomas Malone conducted some studies that offer insight into why this might be the case.[1] By comparing the IQ of individuals to the IQ of groups composed of the same individuals, the researchers discovered a remarkable and strong correlation: the higher the ratio of women to men in a group, the higher the collective IQ of the group. Their theory of causation is not the lack of a Y chromosome. Instead, they believe that the women in their study brought more collaborative skills to the exercise, whereas the "macho" types tended to act like a boss and dictate an answer.

Woolley and Malone's conclusion makes complete sense to me. Brian Marsh, an engineering manager at Google responsible for a substantial part of Google Apps' and Google+'s success, says that a team lead "needs to learn to move at the speed of N, where N is the size of the team." The women in the study were able to reach a consensus that was smarter than they were individually, and the men weren't. In other words, their collaborative approach generates a product name that's better than "Google Turbo."

Put another way, in an old-style compromise between you and a teammate, both of you win 50%, but both of you also you lose 50%. Alternatively, if you and your teammate can work together to reach a creative consensus that achieves your collective goals, 100% of you win and you have achieved what the women-influenced groups in the study achieved—a smarter outcome than either of the individual solutions.

Your goal, therefore, is to facilitate a creative solution that meets the needs of all parties. The Harvard Negotiation Project, popularized by Roger Fisher and William Ury in their book *Getting to Yes* (Penguin), identified the first key step in this process, which is to agree on the objectives.

Let's pretend that I want to use your address book service in my Hello World application. I ask nicely, and you say no initially, because you're already underprovisioned and you don't have additional capacity in your servers. I bet this is feeling familiar, right?

You and I can state and agree upon the objectives that we have in this conflict:

---

1   *http://hbr.org/2011/06/defend-your-research-what-makes-a-team-smarter-more-women/ar/1*

- You don't want your servers to fail because of my requests.
- Your existing clients can't have a decrease of service quality as a result of my usage.
- I need to use your address book service and get good service quality.
- Neither of us wants to be a jerk.

These objectives seem pretty reasonable, and because we agreed that they were reasonable, we started from a point of consensus. Now we can work through each objective to invent a number of solutions that meet all the criteria, such as locally caching address book data on my servers, adding more capacity to your fleet, or building in support for HTTP 503 messages with a response field that points to a read-only version of the database, etc. Inventing a win-win solution that meets the needs of all parties is one of the most important and satisfying parts of being in a leadership role, and should inspire you to embrace negotiations as opportunities for invention.

Sometimes you'll get stuck in your negotiation before you can even discuss the objectives. When this happens, there are three techniques that I've seen help get the negotiation back on track:

- **Focus on facilitation.** Don't start by trying to solve the problem. If you start trying to solve the problem, you take on a point of view and become an interested party, which can make the discussion more complicated. Instead, start by making sure that everyone gets heard. Pay attention to the extroverts, who tend to speak a lot, and the introverts, who are less willing to speak in a group but must be heard when they do speak.
- **"Seek first to understand, then to be understood."** Personal growth guru Stephen Covey authored this principle in his book *The Seven Habits of Highly Effective People* (Free Press), and it's profoundly true. I've found that some of the most influential people in an organization are also some of the worst communicators and are under more pressure (time and otherwise) than is reasonable. Therefore, you have to work incredibly hard to figure out what the other party is really saying. Ask yourself, what does he or she really care about? Then confirm your assumption with questions.

  Frank Patterson, dean of the Florida State University College of Motion Picture Arts, once taught me a nice model for working with actors that applies here. Before trying to offer direction to an actor, articulate what you see by saying, "What I hear you saying is..." By reflecting the message back to the messenger, you give that person the ability to correct you and you minimize communication failures. This is a great technique that emphasizes your desire to seek first to understand, then to be understood.

- **If you already have a bias, go ahead and put it out there and then let others speak.** I think that when the other party is already aware of your beliefs, it makes sense to start by stating your objectives and then pass the baton to the other party so that you can listen. This approach is genuine and efficient.

Up to now, we've focused on negotiation and collaboration in general, but there's a common scenario that requires a slightly more specific set of skills: financial negotiations. Sooner or later, you're going to do a deal for real money, not your *Monopoly* money stock. Your first deal, or even your 1,000th deal, can be intimidating, particularly if you own the company and it's your money you're going to spend. However, nearly all deals are pretty straightforward even though they feel fraught with craziness. I've done quite a few of these deals, including two corporate acquisitions at Google, and I've learned that negotiating financial transactions is like grieving: there are stages, and if you understand them you can better cope with your life and the outcome of the deal.

STAGE 1: IT'S NOT ABOUT YOU

Financial negotiations are nearly always guaranteed to be frustrating because the corporate media elite built up high-powered negotiations as a way of establishing self-worth in the business world. If you believe that your value as a human is a function of your ability to get a fractionally lower recurring service fee from your bandwidth provider, then I'm sorry for your family. Please seek counseling before reading further.

If you see this syndrome in the party you're negotiating with...once again, I'm sorry. Quit now or accept that if there's a perfect middle of the deal, you're not going to end up there. You're going to have to give this macho a-hole his or her pound of flesh if you want to move forward. Accept it and get on with your life. I find it helpful to remind myself that his or her marriage probably stinks.

If you don't believe me that financial deals are excessively macho and media-based, look at the typical phrases used in deal making:

- "It's time to open up the kimono some more."
- "We showed you ours, now let's see yours."
- "Are we going to go to the dance together?"
- "Eventually we have to stop dancing and get down to business."

Yuck! Do yourself a favor and avoid warning-level offenses: don't use these icky aphorisms. If you find someone using them, let such phrases be a reminder to you that he or she is in stage 1. Ask the individual to stop and move on to stage 2.

STAGE 2: BEING FAIR AND USING DATA

Now that you've put away the "I have to get the lowest possible price because that's what Gordon Gekko would do" attitude, you can go about negotiating reasonably. The most reasonable way to negotiate a number is by trading data. For example, you volunteer some data: "I can get bandwidth from AT&T for $1/Gb." Then the other party will volunteer additional data: "Our costs are $0.95 per Gb."

Hopefully things end nicely at this point, settling at $0.98 or $0.97 per gigabit (depending on who's more of an a-hole), and both parties win. Your provider gets a tiny margin and you get a tiny discount.

If only most negotiations were this way! Unfortunately, you're probably saying, "I'm willing to pay $0.75," and they are probably saying, "We need to charge you $1.25." You're not done yet. You're only entering stage 3.

STAGE 3: THAT DATA DIDN'T CLOSE THE DEAL...
LET'S MAKE UP NEW DATA!

The reality is that financial negotiations can take a very long time because you or your counterpart are constantly disclosing and inventing new information. It's the inventing information bit that's particularly challenging. You may invent your build costs: "It'll cost me five engineers for a year to build this, so I shouldn't pay more than $1 million."

Once you cross this line, and you will, the other party will then likewise invent information: "Yes, but your time to market will be accelerated by six months, and that's worth at least $5 million, so you should be willing to pay at least $4 million."

This phase will eventually pass, but in the meantime it's a handwaving arms race, trying to figure out on which side of the middle you will land. Accept that you have to go through this phase and try to get through it quickly.

STAGE 4: SEARCHING FOR THINGS THAT ARE FREE TO GIVE

Eventually, both parties are sick to death of arguing over how many engineers for how many months it will take to integrate, or how much each customer is really worth, or how long it will take Microsoft, Google, or Apple to build competing technology. In stage 4, each party tries to throw worthless crap that costs little to give into the deal. "We have major launch plans," you say, "we'll put you on the stage at Moscone Center." The other side won't even bother to put a value on this marketing ploy, and the reality is that you shouldn't expect them to do so; you're just hoping that if you "sweeten the deal" enough, they'll take the last number you offered in stage 3.

In many ways, this "deal sweetening" phase is time that each party spends trying to get comfortable with The Reality Of The Situation, which is that neither of you is going to make out like a bandit. It's too bad, but we always feel disappointed at this point, even though bandits are the bad guys—except in movies, where "corporate raider" sounds glamorous (see stage 1).

STAGE 5: WALKING AWAY AND THINKING

It's possible that after throwing in a few pot sweeteners and a few months of negotiation, everyone is so tired that you're ready to do a deal. So you just do it. If this is you, proceed to stage 6 and light a candle at the chapel on the way home. Also, some money to the Salvation Army Santa might be in order.

Most of us are not so lucky because fatigue makes everything worse (or so my new-mother friends tell me). It's possible that stage 1 (in which you wanted to be Gordon Gekko, master of the universe) may rear its ugly head again. Posturing may ensue: "OK, we're too far apart; I guess we'll have to build it ourselves." Threats may be made: "We're going to put you out of business anyway..." Phones may be put on mute and warning-offense quality curses uttered.

It's at this point that a necessary cooling-off period is introduced organically. One party walks away from the deal, or gets upset and stops returning calls, or whatever. This is a good thing for the process because both parties get distance from the negotiation and return to being close to their products. This newly created distance allows you to consider again The Reality Of The Situation.

The products are where the deal started. You want them and they want you. If you really can't live with the other party's terms from a business standpoint, then yes, walk away. If you can live with the terms, then you're going to have to take them. Give the discussion a couple of weeks to cool off and start over at stage 2, in which you share data. Stage 2 will play out differently this time because you'll be willing to share more data and pay more money. The other party will also share more and be willing to take less, and you will all be somewhat more motivated to reach a number that is acceptable.

STAGE 6: AGREEMENT, PAPERWORK, AND RECRIMINATIONS

Just when you thought you were done, you'll discover that any reasonably valuable deal is going to require a lot of paperwork. It's not the paperwork that's the problem. The problem is that there are tiny details inside the paperwork that can bring you right back to stage 5 and have you plotting scorched-earth solutions to this deal. These details exist because any contract that's going to be effective needs to be extremely clear. To add clarity you must define every detail, and it is at this point that you discover miscommunication—and miscommunication leads to conflict.

If both parties are exhausted and macho, the deal will go off the rails at this point, in the same way that a mythical quarter can derail Amtrak. Remind yourself that this is merely a quarter, not the whole $10 million stack of bills, and let it go if at all possible. Employ the techniques for dealing with conflict that are described later in this chapter, and work hard to get the train back on the rails. You have, after all, "agreed to go to the dance" with these people, so be the bigger person and eat at the restaurant at which they want to eat.

Months later, you and your deal team probably won't care about how much you paid. Over a beer, all you'll remember is how long it took to do the deal. You may look back and say, "Why the heck did that take so long?!?" The answer is that most of the time was spent on stages 1, 3, 4, 5, and 6. Yep, these are the steps that were not based on hard data. So, if there's a moral to the story, it's *don't be macho*.

Dealing with Conflict

The third and final tool you need to reach a great consensus is conflict management. We can assert from the start that there are a lot of a-holes out there, and they breed conflict. You may even think you work with a unique nexus of a-holes, idiots, and self-absorbed twits. But because you're in the software industry, the odds are really quite small that this is the case. The odds are much better that the people you work with have subnormal communication skills and supernormal technical skills.

"But wait," you may be saying, "I work with product managers and engineering VPs and designers—they certainly can't have bad communication skills!" Ergo, they must be a-holes. You might be right. More likely, these people are so used to dealing with engineers and folks like you that they're desperately insecure and afraid that you're going to randomize their efforts. These people also care about shipping. Perhaps they care less about shipping than you do, but they care enough to be afraid that you're going to alter their designs, objectives, or question their decisions in such a way that you'll spark a reset.

Tony Schwartz is a management guru who wrote that in situations like this, you need to tell yourself a different story.[2] The story he's talking about is the explanation you create for yourself to explain someone's bizarre behavior. But it's just that: a story, and it's created from assumptions. Instead of assuming that the other person in this conflict is an a-hole, consider telling yourself a different story.

I'll give you an example. When I joined the Maps team at Google, I was really frustrated by the design team. They seemed sharp and nice, but I was constantly butting heads with them when I asked normal questions like "What is the user problem you are trying to solve?" They would respond with, "Our design goal is 'the map is the UI.' You really need to spend more time with the other product managers."

I was inclined to believe the Maps designers were idiots because "the map is the UI" is not a design goal and it doesn't help users. But late into a whining rant over a bottle of white Côtes du Rhône, a designer friend of mine suggested a different story. "They've had no business goal," she said. "Instead, they've been getting random complaints for years and since they've had no business goals, they've had to try to do your job on their own. They invented an organizing principle that could absorb all these tiny complaints from random VPs. And they may see you as just another one of those VPs."

It's not every day that your friends will give you brilliant insight, I know. But you can effect the same outcome, and save some bank on the vino, by saying, "OK, I'm telling myself the story that they're idiots. I don't actually have the IQ scores to back that up. Perhaps the story is that the

2   http://hbr.org/2007/10/manage-your-energy-not-your-time/ar/1

former VP gave them a horrible objective, and they're trying to live to it—in which case, it makes sense that they're defending it."

If you change the story you're telling yourself about the other party, you can internally position yourself to have a more positive response to a conflict.

Now that you've convinced yourself that the guy you're dealing with might not be an a-hole, you can get to the root of the problem. About 90% of the time, the root cause for your conflict is miscommunication. The other 10% of the time is divided between 1% genuine a-holes and 9% misaligned objectives.

All you really need to understand is that 90% of the time, you and your counterpart are "talking past each other." In other words, you agree about the important things and are getting hung up on some detail or language problem. I find that engineers and engineering managers frequently focus on details when they really care about something much bigger, like not writing duplicate code, because it's easier to be specific about a detail. By understanding that you're most likely talking past each other, you can take a step back and ask yourself what the other party is really trying to say. This is the first major step.

Once you've established that you're talking past each other, you can use that opportunity to establish a common vocabulary for the discussion so you can avoid miscommunication that results from language problems. To do this, you need to understand that engineers and teams frequently imbue certain words with special meaning. On one team a "hack" might be a horrible, dangerous thing, while on another team a "hack" might be a nice shortcut. Or, as I learned on the Maps team at Google, a common word like "landmark" might represent a whole class of things (restaurants, hotels, and the Eiffel Tower), rather than just the Eiffel Tower, which was referred to as an "attraction." Such generalizations and naming conventions are *de rigueur* in software because that's how software works—it operates on abstract objects and applies properties to make them specific. Therefore, it's extremely common and entirely reasonable for teams to develop their own language.

Luckily, it's simple to get past taxonomy problems. Say, "I'm sorry—so we're on the same page, what are you referring to when you say 'landmark'?" Engineering teams will be happy to explain because they love defining things. It's one of the reasons why they write code.

If you are both using the same words with the same meaning, you may be "talking past each other" because one of you doesn't understand the context of the conversation fully. Most of the nonengineers you work with are spread very thin across many projects. They do not necessarily know why you're discussing a topic, and you don't necessarily know why they are being a jerk. Take a step back and say, "I think we might be talking past each other." Then get, or give, the context. For example:

> Just for context, and so we're all on the same page, maybe I can give a little background? We're trying to build an application that does text-to-speech for blind users. Unfortunately, we want to ship at the Consumer Electronics Show, and that means we have a hard deadline. And, because our target user is blind, we have to make some tough decisions and optimizations. Does that make sense so far?

This example reveals two critical and common contextual elements. First, time is always a challenge, and clearly articulating the time constraints will help the other person understand what is possible. Don't believe me that time is a problem? Have a friend tie two moderately complicated knots. Then, you and another friend untie the knots while blindfolded and not speaking. Repeat this task but with a one-minute limit. The difference between the two experiences is remarkable, and you probably encountered some frustrating, nonverbal conflict because although it's initially challenging to communicate while blindfolded and mute, everything gets worse under time pressure.

The second dimension that the example shows is that there are frequently assumptions that other people make or don't know about. In this example, the design target is a blind user, and that user has different needs than a typical text-to-speech user. When you provide context to teammates, be sure to tease out these assumptions because they frequently lead to miscommunication.

On a related note, try to keep your project name the same throughout the life of the product, because if you change it, you'll confuse the people who didn't hear about the name change. If you're in a tiny company, changing the name doesn't matter, but it does in a big company. Renaming a project rarely delivers enough benefit to make dealing with the resulting miscommunication worthwhile. And it will increase your Excedrin bill.

When words are failing you, and your attempts to clarify them through taxonomy and context are also met with hostility and dismay, turn to the whiteboard. I always have a big whiteboard by my desk for this reason. I've found that pictures and lists drive clarity. By writing down what you're talking about, the other party can focus on the pictures or the words on the board, rather than words in the air. This is a simple technique, but it's remarkably powerful.

There are times, however, when conflict is not the result of explicit miscommunication or fundamentally divergent viewpoints. Sometimes conflict occurs when someone pokes you in a place you don't like being poked. You'll know when you get poked because you either want to slug the bastard or run away. You had a classic fight-or-flight response.

When someone pokes you in a way that triggers you, take a full minute to understand what just happened. Stall. Say, "Huh." It takes 60 seconds for the initial bolus of adrenaline to be absorbed into your system after you've been poked, and 20 minutes for that adrenaline to be completely absorbed. Therefore, doing absolutely nothing but stalling for 60 seconds gives you time to avoid running from the room or from poking that person right back.

If you want to get better at coping with the strong emotional responses we all have, you need to identify what triggers such a response. Maybe people who use your childhood nickname upset you, or maybe engineers who question your technical judgment really get your goat. Regardless of what the specific trigger is, being aware that you were poked in a sensitive place will give you the handle you need to wrestle your reactions back into shape, and over time your sensitivity will decrease.

Even if you can manage your triggers, it's clear that working on software is an intense business that will occasionally cause tempers to flare. Most people work longer-than-average days and care passionately about the work they produce. It's not surprising that emotions are strong, and you'd best accept right now that you're going to piss someone off, especially if you're trying to ship. But you may be able to minimize the frequency with which you piss people off if you can depersonalize your conversations.

Depersonalizing conversations means making the discussion about the software, the user, or the problem—not about the humans involved in the conversation. There are some powerful techniques you can employ every day to help ensure that you depersonalize your discussions and increase the probability of a stressless outcome. My top three favorite depersonalization techniques are:

- Don't say "You" or "I."
- Focus on the persona, not the people.
- Use objective measures.

DON'T USE "YOU" OR "I"

Try removing all instances of the words "You" and "I" from email. This technique depersonalizes the correspondence and focuses statements on the product rather than on what "you" think or what "I" contributed. If you can bring yourself to remove "you" and "I" from verbal communications, do that as well. You may find that you write in the passive voice more often, but it is a small price to pay to reduce your team's stress levels and increase their happiness. Google is such a strong supporter of this approach that members of promotion committees are not allowed to say, "I think..." Instead, the committee member is supposed to say, "The promotion packet indicates..." Similarly, parliamentary protocol doesn't allow politicians to speak directly to one another, which adds a layer of buffer and helps make the arguments less personal.

FOCUS ON THE PERSONAS, NOT THE PEOPLE

Another powerful way of talking about problems is to use personas like you might use sock puppets. Sock puppets have stood the test of time because they depersonalize challenging conversations, and personas can do the same thing. For example, instead of saying, "You don't really want to sign in first, what you want to do is find out if the product is in stock..." you might say, "Sarah Shopper is a shopper. She wants to look around and evaluate her options. What does she want to do?"

Talking through Sarah Shopper depersonalized the conversation substantially. What's more, personas are effective when it comes to making hard decisions, because the person who will get the short end of the stick when you cut that special feature is the persona, not the person who invented it. To continue our example, you might say something like, "We've said that Sarah is more important than Stanley. So we will need to optimize for Sarah here."

USE OBJECTIVE MEASURES

When I interview product managers and ask them to tell me about a time when they had to change someone's mind, they almost always talk about how they used facts to turn someone around. They rarely get hired because their stories inevitably end badly. It's sad, but the real world doesn't care much about facts. You can see evidence for this trend in the Fox News "I don't have the facts to back this up" approach to reporting. If you're going to live in a world where facts play second fiddle to opinions, you're going to need a way to deal with opinions as if they are facts. Luckily, we have *usability tests* and *decision matrices*.

Usability tests are great for establishing whether a subjective experience—user interface—succeeds or fails. You can read more about usability tests in Chapter 3.

A decision matrix is a simple chart that you build to help you decide between options. Table 11-1 demonstrates a decision matrix that will help me choose a pet.

Table 11-1. Pet decision matrix

Criteria/animal	Cat	Dog	Rabbit
Doesn't shed	0	2	1
Cuddly	1	0	2
Friendly	1	2	0
Total	2	4	3

Clearly I should get a dog. When you establish a set of criteria by which the team will evaluate options and then evaluate those options as a team, you will craft a transparent picture of what your goals and priorities are. In addition, because the team can weigh in on each dimension, the discussion can focus on much more granular elements so no one is losing everything. Put another way, if I think "dogs are definitely a 1 on the cuddly scale," and you think "nothing that drools like a dog can ever be cuddly, it's a 0," you and I are much more likely to be able to reach a consensus than we would if we were debating whether cats or dogs are better, because the worst case for both of us is that dogs are overappreciated or underappreciated by one point. That's very different than an argument about whether dogs are better than cats.

It's good to go a step further in your decision matrices if you have time. If you add a "weight" or "priority" column, as shown in Table 11-2, the team will have to discuss and agree upon the relative importance of various decision criteria. This process is immensely valuable for getting your team on the same page. In your case, you might have to compare reduced development time, increased scalability, and increased testability, all of which are good and important things, but you can't get scalability and testability without spending more development time! In my case, I really don't want an animal that sheds.

Table 11-2. Decision matrix with weights

Criteria/animal	Weight	Cat	Dog	Rabbit
Doesn't shed	2	0	2	1
Cuddly	1	1	0	2
Friendly	1.5	1	2	0
Total		2.5	7	4

Good. Snoopy can stay.

12

How to Stay a Great Person While Shipping

I TRIED HARD TO come up with a way to sugarcoat this but I couldn't, so here's the bombshell: shipping great software is damn hard and crazy stressful. It's also incredibly rewarding. The energy you spend is worth it. But the stresses placed on those called upon to ship can be extreme. Sometimes you'll be asked to balance multiple competing priorities without guidance. You may be asked to do the job of three people in half the time it would take one. And throughout the project you'll probably have to deal with feature requests, changing corporate priorities, politics, and general unfairness. But wait—there's more! There's hope!

There are tricks that can help you cope with these shipping life challenges. I've spent many years working with colleagues who were all trying to ship, and there's a small kernel of battle-hardened advice that I've gathered and held on to. I think it helps, and it's broken down into these five categories:

- How to balance shipping, quality and impact, and your team, so you deliver great software.
- How to handle *randomization*, so you can continue to ship a great product in a timely way. Randomization is what happens when your management throws you a curveball, or your team wanders off into the weeds. Randomization is one of those words that everyone at Google and Amazon understands because it's the opposite of helping a team stay focused on shipping.
- How to manage your energy deliberately, so you can do the job of three people.
- How and when to escalate, so the right work gets done by the right people.
- How to eat the s#!@ sandwich, because sometimes, you're just gonna have to.

How to Balance Shipping, Quality and Impact, and Your Team

Let's pretend you're the CEO for a moment. (If you are the CEO, please buy copies of this book for everyone at your company.) If your team lead happily announces to the world that your new product is ready, and it's actually a steaming pile, you wouldn't consider that team or that team lead successful. Neither would I. That lead is fired.

If your lead, through charisma or knowledge of dark secrets, manages to ship something pretty good quickly but leaves behind a burned-out, disheartened team, you would also consider that a failure and sack that person. If you don't, the board is going to fire *you*.

If your lead, in a fit of aggressive cost cutting and schedule pressure, reduces the feature so much that you have no bugs and the team can ship early, but users don't care about the product, the lead is fired.

A successful team lead must balance team, quality and impact, and a desire to always be shipping. As you work through the different phases of your shipping process and the details in this book, remember this balance (shown in Figure 12-1). Maintain it, and you will remain employed. Understanding that you can't have perfection in all dimensions, but that you *can* have balance, will help you manage your shipping life. You also now have tools you can employ to see if you are out of balance, like the vibe in your weekly team meeting, the High School Embarrassment Test, and your product requirements document: are you still solving a big problem that lots of people share?

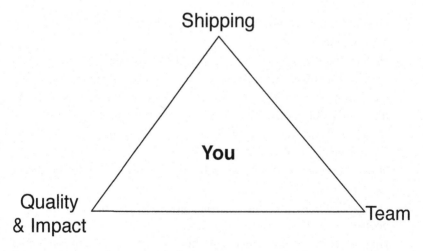

Figure 12-1. The shipping balance triangle

How to Handle Randomization

Since you're not the boss, and life isn't fair, your product will probably suffer from a constant stream of well-intentioned but nonetheless disruptive suggestions. Unfortunately, as your product becomes more important and your deadline grows closer, the volume of suggestions will increase, because your software will get more visibility through the dogfood process. You can't eliminate these suggestions, but you can stop them from distracting or "randomizing" the team. Randomization feels like you were on stage 2 when someone rolled an 18-sided die and said, "Go do stage 13 instead."

It's generally not your fault when this happens. There are many sources of randomization. Feature requests are common. Corporate priorities may shift. And you may even be forced to accept some substantial infrastructure change. You have to take this randomization in stride and try to continue with business as usual.

To deal with feature requests, create a simple, shared document into which you'll aggregate them. Make this document public to everyone because transparency will reduce fear-based concerns and the volume of incoming questions. When someone suggests a new feature, say, "Thank you sooooo much! I added your idea to our feature requests; here is a link." This technique works like the technique you apply in meetings, where you write everything your team says on the whiteboard; writing down the feedback is an explicit form of acknowledgment (but not commitment).

When randomizing suggestions come from management or investors, you can help defuse the suggestions with the Version 1 test. Ask, "Would you block the Version 1 launch on it?" In some cases, you'll hear an unequivocal "yes," and you'll be scared right to the marrow of your bones. Don't freak out yet—there's still hope.

When the founder or the board says, "Yes, it must be in V1," your next step is to pull your development lead aside to share what's going on. Ask the lead to figure out what the engineering impact of the change will be. You want to assess the cost in terms of engineering weeks, systems design, capacity, and any other functions on which you depend, like legal. If the estimate is small, don't worry about it and add the feature. The exception to this rule is when you're very close to launch and the "just say no" protocol is in effect (see Chapter 7). If the cost estimate generated by your development lead is large, go back to your senior management with the estimate and ask, "Are you willing to block the launch for six weeks and buy 100 more computers for this feature, or can we add it to the immediately post-launch list?" At this point, you can have a real, rational conversation about cost and benefit. There is no point in pushing back on a requirement until you have an estimate of costs, unless the requirement is evil.

If the suggestion is really wacky, and also must be in V1, sometimes the best thing to do is not fight the suggestion. If it's a terrible idea, your trusted testers will tell you, and your senior management will have a very hard time arguing with vocal customers and user data. In situations like these, you can work with your team to invest a minimum of engineering effort, deploy the feature as quickly as possible to your trusted testers, and then wait and see. You might be wrong, but if you're not, bring the data back to your management and go from there.

Listening well in your review meetings can help you avoid some randomization. Remember, if the Big Boss says you should do something, you probably need to do it. If you fail to either tackle this head-on with that manager or fail to deliver on expectations, you'll be randomized. It is a mistake to assume that your bosses will forget the requirement they communicated; if you've taken verbatim notes in your meetings, you'll know precisely what expectations are and you can manage to them. Doing so will substantially decrease your odds of being randomized.

There are, of course, sources of randomization you can't control, like changing corporate priorities. Diving deep into the tricks and tips for dealing with corporate politics is beyond the scope of this book. It seems to me that some people are innately good at dealing with politics, and others don't have a political bone in their body. I fall into the latter group, so I can only offer four basic coping strategies, in sequential order, for dealing with shifting corporate priorities. Remember, your goal is to ship, so you want the engineering team to carry on as if nothing has changed:

1. **Find out if the priority change is real.** Sometimes leaders state that priorities are shifting, but the company has no intention of following through or lacks the ability to do so. The people who will know if the changes are real are generally only one level removed from the people who initiated the change. Talk to these one-level-removed individuals and get their honest assessment, one-on-one, and not in writing. You may hear something different than the party line, and find out that the senior leadership is trying to appease some external group. You may even hear that the decision isn't final yet. If this is the case, you can carry on as usual, and you're done coping. For now.

2. **Recast your product to align.** In some cases, you can easily recast your product so it aligns with the new priorities without actually changing your engineering work. Rework your short presentation and see if acknowledging that you understand the new world order gives you and your team room to breathe. If it does, you can carry on as usual.

3. **Change as little as possible.** If you want to carry on as usual and ship, and you must take a change, you need to make the smallest change you can possibly make. The bigger the change you take, the greater the randomization you will experience and the greater the risk to your launch. Work with your engineering team to find a low-cost quick win. Generally doing something small and quick proves that your team is paying attention and buys you enough time to ship. In fact, if you can be the first to show reasonable progress conforming to the new priorities, you may buy your team disproportionate leeway to proceed at your own pace, since you've made it clear that you will get the job done. Make the small change, and you're back to business as usual.

4. **Ask for an exception.** Sometimes asking for an exception can be the best way to move forward. Getting a wholesale exception is particularly important if the only way to move forward involves major ship-stopping changes. A variant of asking for an exception is asking to respond to the new corporate priorities in Version 2. Explain the cost of responding to the new priorities in the same way you would when the Big Boss asks for a change. If you get an exception and can push the changes into V2, you're done. Once again, carry on as usual.

5. **Suck it up.** If you try all of these techniques and make no headway, I'm sorry. You're in a tough situation, and this is one of those s#!@ sandwich–eating times, which we will cover soon. Eat the sandwich and write a new product requirements document. Remember to reset your milestones—it would be deeply unfair to your team to forget to do so.

All of these coping strategies apply to big infrastructure changes, too. There's one additional rule of thumb for working with infrastructure on which you depend: you want to be in the middle of the train. Infrastructure projects steam into town like a big, screeching train. It takes a long time to start these kinds of projects, and they're loud, pushy, and obnoxious for the most part. If you're right at the front of the train, an early adopter of the infrastructure, you're going to run into bugs, cows, and the occasional Karmann Ghia—none of which is fun. You don't want to be an early adopter of a major infrastructure project.

On the flipside, if you're the caboose you'll likely get whiplashed. Your management will ask, "Why aren't you done with porting to X yet?" Your systems will likely start to break in funny ways. Support for your old infrastructure will become obsolete, and you'll generally be in an uncomfortable place. You don't want to be at the tail end of the train.

You want to be in the middle of the train—right near the club car where they keep the cocktails and pretzels. Find two to three other teams whose progress you can monitor. When you see a team go through the process of switching to the new infrastructure relatively painlessly, it is time to start switching to the new infrastructure. The documentation for the new infrastructure is probably decent at this point, but you can also ask that successful team to guide you through the switch. The guidance you get from users is almost always better than the guidance you'll get from the infrastructure developers.

How to Manage Your Energy While Shipping

One Amazon engineering manager I know once spent only 20 minutes building an important presentation for an executive review. This was unlike him, but he'd been fighting production fires all week. I turned in my chair and said, "Really, that's it?" And he shrugged. "Time to go," he said.

A half-hour later, he came back from the meeting, sat down, and said, "Well, I spent the right amount of time on *that* deck." This was a seminal moment in my career because it taught me that I must learn how much time was the right amount of time to spend on each task. In this case, he was pretty sure that the execs had already made up their minds, so why bother spending a lot of time on a presentation when he'd only get to the first slide? There are many things you need to do if you're going to ship, most of which are described in detail in this book, but you won't be able to do all of them.

Kim Rachmeler, the former VP of Worldwide Discovery at Amazon, once said to me, "When I hired the first program manager into Amazon, I sat her next to me and every day I would get up from my desk and say, 'That's another day where I didn't get everything done,' because I wanted

her to understand that the work of a program manager is never done—
what's important is doing what had to be done today."

Since you can't do everything that the team needs, you need to do the
right stuff, and be OK with not getting everything done. Peter Drucker
echoes this sentiment in *The Effective Executive*. He says that the things
you should do first are the things that you, and only you, can do. Working
in this way will help you maximize your effectiveness and prevent you
from becoming a blocker.

One small example of how this works well at Google is that there's
a culture of very fast expense report approvals. Good managers understand that they are the critical blocker on that one task, so they deal with
it immediately.

I used to worry more about my energy. So I asked Eric Schmidt how
we planned to help product managers who were burning the candle at
both ends stay at the company. Eric said, "I think many product managers
are initially inefficient in their time management." I was chagrined—I
thought I was doing a pretty good job, and I was definitely feeling stretched
pretty thin! In hindsight, when I look at the volume of work that Eric
completed, and contrast that with how I've learned to prioritize doing the
things that only I can do first, spend the right amount of time on any given
task, and be OK with not getting everything done, I think he was right.

If you're having a tough time learning to be efficient with your time
and your energy, or recognize that this is a skill you are completely missing, consider learning from Tony Schwartz's Energy Project.[1] Schwartz
wrote a great Harvard Business Review article entitled "Managing Your
Energy, Not Your Time" and subsequently developed a book and a whole
business around the notion of optimizing your personal energy.[2] He's a
major advocate of understanding where you spend energy, how to optimize where you spend it, and how to establish greater reserves of it. Many
effective executives are beginning to adopt his approach because it really
works. It's a bit crazy, what with some CEOs keeping pillows in their offices, but it seems effective.

A final trick you can employ to help manage your energy is schedul-
ing time to work. Because you're trying to ship, most, if not all, of your
time is consumed with meetings. This means that you have little time

---

1   *http://www.theenergyproject.com/*

2   *http://hbr.org/2007/10/manage-your-energy-not-your-time/ar/1*

to write a product requirements document, review the user experience, and talk with your engineering team about your systems design. And for some strange and wonderful reason, people who would otherwise book your calendar solid until late at night are unlikely to book over your "work time." Tony Schwartz would suggest that you schedule the first hour and a half in the morning to make progress against your hardest task. An hour and a half is a nice amount of time to work intently before taking a break, and the morning is when most of us have our best energy. Generally, your hardest task is also your least reactive and the task you're most likely to postpone, so if you're a procrastinator, using this scheduled time is a nice way of pushing through. It's worth trying, right?

How to Use Escalation as a Tool, Not an Excuse

We've established that you're not the boss—but somebody, somewhere, is. That bossypants can be a valuable asset! Knowing when to escalate is a key skill, just like "over" is a key part of "over, under, and through," which you should have learned in kindergarten.

You probably want to escalate when any of the following conditions is met:

- **You're trying to defend an otherwise silly executive mandate.** You shouldn't have to stand up for bad ideas. You might have to in the long run, but do your best to make the bosses defend their bad ideas.
- **You honestly don't understand why you should do something.** In situations like this, it's best to get an explanation one-on-one because the Big Boss will likely be more transparent. If you ask for an explanation over email, don't cc the team.
- **It's not your responsibility to solve the problem.** One of the classic times when you need to escalate is when your engineering team is making a decision you think has dubious technical merit. Most leaders with an engineering background have good enough instincts that they know when the train is going off the rails. Rather than trying to go head-to-head with your tech lead, let the engineering manager with the legitimate authority, and the responsibility, deal with the engineering team. In addition, taking the engineering team's side in this manager-staff crisis can help you build equity with the team.

  I think it's important to point out that I'm not advocating that you eschew all responsibility for things that aren't purely in your job function. If there's something you can fix, and your team is willing to have you fix it, fix it! Be proactive and assertive in your fixes, and don't let your title or job description limit you. But when you get into a situation where there's a problem that is someone else's responsibility to fix—and that person would be unhappy with you fixing it instead—escalate.

- **You're dealing with senior managers who don't want to listen.** They may not be listening to you because you don't rank high enough or, more likely, because they don't know you. However, your management or investors probably have an existing relationship with the troublesome senior managers. They're in meetings (read: golf) together frequently and have developed trust. Leveraging the trust and understanding that your management has built rapport with other executives is an efficient way to lead.

How to Eat the S#!@ Sandwich and Survive

There's no way around it: you are going to need to eat a certain number of s#!@ sandwiches as you try to ship your product. Some of these sandwiches come from partners. Some come from your bosses or investors. Some come from whiny engineers or competition. You need to accept right now that there are times when your life as a team lead is going to really suck.

I once worked on a project at Amazon and had a crisis in which my senior management freaked out. It was painful. Customers were sending email to Jeff, and you never hear about the thank-you notes they send, only the rants.

The thing that helped me survive this near-career-apocalypse was what the guy sitting next to me said as I waited for the VP to come down the elevator and deliver my special sandwich. My colleague said, "This is going to suck for a while, but then it'll be over." That stuck with me, and I've said it to others many times—probably more times than I care to remember.

You can think of these sandwiches like high school. Surviving them is the point. Your goal, when offered a sandwich, is to keep smiling, eat the sandwich, and move on. Matt Glotzbach, a product management director at Google and one of the coolest cucumbers in the patch, once said to me, "The time to keep your cool is when everyone else is losing theirs." So eat the sandwich, keep smiling, and remember what it felt like so that you're less inclined to prepare those sandwiches and hand them to your team.

There is one small caveat in my deli advice. In some bad environments, you may find that you're eating these sandwiches all day, every day. This is a bad sign. William Gibson, author of the cyberpunk pioneering book *Neuromancer* (Ace) and understander of tech culture extraordinaire, once said, "Before you diagnose yourself with depression or low self-esteem, first make sure that you are not, in fact, just surrounding yourself with assholes." Sometimes the volume and quality of the sandwiches you are required to eat is a direct product of the assholes you're working with. When this is the case, it's time to go ship something else, somewhere else.

13

That Was Great;
Let's Do It Again

WHEN YOU'VE BEEN THROUGH the drama, pain, and rigor of a major product development cycle, it's easy to see only your software's deficiencies. But if pilots can say, "The best landing is the one you walk away from," you can say the same thing about your software. The software that ships is the best software. Shipping is the point. So what happens after you ship?

Aaron Abrams, a program manager at REI.com, says, "There are two great days for a program manager: the day you get your project and the day you ship it." Hopefully you celebrated the day after you shipped your project (see Chapter 7). You're now ready for the other great day—the day you get your next project.

Before you start your next project, take a step back and look at the environment around you. Software is never complete. You need to ask yourself if you should start work on V2 or start something new. At some point, you will start to experience a law of diminishing returns on your investment in a product. The investment I'm talking about is your time. Your capital, the venture capital of time, is one of the most leveraged assets you have.

If you're any good at all—and if you can execute according to the guidance in this book, you will be—you will always have options for your next project. Consider what the options mean to your business and to you personally. It may be time to work with a new team or on a new product. Maybe you need to rebuild the product you just shipped, because you misunderstood what customers needed. Or maybe you simply love working with that engineering manager pal of yours. There are dozens of dimensions to evaluate, and it will take you some time to process them.

All of the skills you brought to bear to define your last product are meaningful at this introspective stage. You can think about the customer problems, your business's unique advantages, and your personal strengths. The right investment for you will likely be personal, and even if your next project is something that's assigned directly to you by someone else, you still have a choice about how you approach it and on what you're going to focus.

A great leader ships the right software, not just anything that comes across his or her desk. If you want to see great personal and professional returns, you must be deliberate about how you invest your time.

After you make a decision about what you will do next, you have to transition to your next project. Aaron Abrams also competes in Ironman triathlons. (An Ironman is one of the few things I'd consider harder than remaining employed while attempting to ship.) He says that "transitions—you know, from the swim to the bike, or the bike to the run—are the hard part." I think any part of an Ironman is hard, but he makes a good point. In software, the transition into a new project is always challenging.

Project transitions are challenging because, just as in Ironman races, you have to stop doing things one way (i.e., operating in detail-focused, prelaunch mode) and start doing things another way (i.e., engaging in brainstorming and strategegy). Transitions are also challenging because you're trying to do two jobs. The first job is maintaining the software that's in production and is almost certainly experiencing some kind of growing pains. The second job is spinning up the new project, and if it's like most projects, it requires a huge amount of activation energy to kick-start and substantial mental toughness to survive the inevitable shin bashing as that kick-starter smacks you.

Being in transition is a tough place to be, so make the transition short. Make it shorter than you think it should be. If you've ever noticed that things at the office go better than you'd expect when you take a long vacation, you'll find that the same is true when you walk away from your old project. The team will probably slow down for a bit. They'll probably do things that make you slap your forehead or make decisions that cause you to groan horribly as you pour your coffee—but it's not your problem anymore. Worse than that, you may see your product, under its new leaders, in a Superbowl ad. This happened to me, and boy, did I second-guess my decision to leave!

All of this drama will eventually disappear because you're shipping something new. You shipped V1 of *their* software, and it's not yours anymore. Wish your former team good luck and get back to work. Check in on your mission and your strategy, and start writing your next press release.

Good luck!

CHRIS VANDER MEY

Seattle, Washington
2012

10 Principles of Shipping

1. You are not the boss—team leads are servants and exist to serve the engineering team.
2. Start with the user and work outward.
3. Solve a hard problem that lots of people share, in a unique way.
4. Bad news is good news (via Jack Welch).
5. Seek first to understand, then to be understood (via Stephen Covey).
6. Build the simplest thing that can possibly work.
7. You ship the software you have, not the software you want.
8. If you cannot measure it, you cannot improve it (via Lord Kelvin).
9. You'll never do the whole job, so first do that which only you can do.
10. Always Be Shipping.

Essential Artifacts Your Team Needs

As you manage your product development, you'll produce many documents, guides, checklists, and other artifacts. This list is a summary of the artifacts you should expect to produce throughout your product life cycle. You will probably need them all, so they're presented in no particular order. You can find templates for some of these artifacts available for download from *www.shippinggreatness.com*.

- An on-call rotation—copied into a wallet-sized list of pagers and cell phone numbers.
- A wiki on "Who to contact" in the case of problems, emergencies, or questions. This should include owners and contact information for legal, PR, marketing, the product team, engineering, and network operations (or whatever your production infrastructure equivalent is).
- A mission statement.
- A clear strategy for the next two years.
- A one-page document that summarizes the who/what/why/when/how of your product.
- A product requirements document, also known as a functional spec.
- A press release.
- Wireframe mocks or napkin sketches.
- An internal FAQ with a subset of questions tagged for an external FAQ as preliminary support content.
- A communications document that covers your key message, potential dangerous questions, and responses to those questions.
- T-shirts for when you launch.
- A development schedule that includes testing time.
- A two-year roadmap.
- For infrastructure projects, an internal customer list and schedule of adoption.

- For externally facing products, a trusted tester list.
- A feature request list, with the top three features requested by customers highlighted (internal and external).
- An open issues list with the status of those open issues clearly marked.
- Ongoing meeting notes. It's nice to have a document that contains all the historical meeting notes for the project.
- A release plan/protocol.
- A production change list of what features were released and when. Very useful when troubleshooting customer problems.
- A production design document that forecasts growth projections and hardware allocation requirements.
- Patent filings, trademark filings, and copyright filings.
- A privacy statement.
- Great metrics—including internal dashboards and a few sanitized metrics for external consumption.
- Screenshots for slides/presentations/reviews/launches.
- Quarterly objectives for your team and previous quarterly objectives with status marked clearly.
- A bug dashboard and list of bugs that block each release.
- Cause of error reports or postmortems.
- Meeting notes and schedules for: your team's weekly meeting, UI review, product review, engineering review, bug triage, legal reviews, weekly business development, and weekly customer support check-ins.

References and Further Reading

Product Definition

Kawasaki, Guy. *The Art of the Start: The Time-Tested, Battle-Hardened Guide for Anyone Starting Anything.* New York: Portfolio Hardcover, 2004.

Ries, Eric. *The Lean Startup: How Today's Entrepreneurs Use Continuous Innovation to Create Radically Successful Businesses.* New York: Crown Business, 2011.

Managing Management

Bossidy, Larry, and Ram Charan. *Execution: The Discipline of Getting Things Done.* New York: Crown Business, 2002.

Drucker, Peter F. *The Effective Executive: The Definitive Guide to Getting the Right Things Done,* Revised Edition. New York: HarperBusiness, 2006.

Fisher, Robert, William L. Ury, and Bruce Patton. *Getting to Yes: Negotiating Without Giving In,* Second Edition. New York: Penguin Books, 1991.

Kotter, John P. *Leading Change.* Boston: Harvard Business School Press, 1996.

Engineering Management

DeMarco, Tom, and Timothy Lister. *Peopleware: Productive People and Teams*, Second Edition. New York: Dorset House, 1999.

UX

Pruitt, John, and Tamara Adlin. *The Persona Lifecycle: Keeping People in Mind Throughout Product Design*. San Francisco: Morgan Kaufmann, 2006.

Tufte, Edward R. *The Visual Display of Quantitative Information*, Second Edition. Cheshire, Connecticut: Graphics Press, 2001.

Williams, Robin. *The Non-Designer's Design Book*, Third Edition. Berkeley, California: Peachpit Press, 2008.

Metrics

Goldratt, Eliyahu M., and Jeff Cox. *The Goal: A Process of Ongoing Improvement*, Third Revised Edition. Great Barrington, Massachusetts: North River Press, 2004.

Communications

De Bono, Edward. *Six Thinking Hats*. Boston: Back Bay Books, 1999.

Schwartz, Tony, and Catherine McCarthy. "Manage Your Energy, Not Your Time." *Harvard Business Review*, October 2007, 63–72. *http://hbr.org/2007/10/manage-your-energy-not-your-time/ar/1*.

How to Contact Us

We'd Like to Hear from You

Please address comments and questions concerning this book to the publisher:

O'Reilly Media, Inc.
1005 Gravenstein Highway North
Sebastopol, CA 95472
(800) 998-9938 (in the United States or Canada)
(707) 829-0515 (international or local)
(707) 829-0104 (fax)

We have a web page for this book, where we list errata, examples, and any additional information. You can access this page at:

http://oreil.ly/shipping_greatness

The author also maintains a website for this book at:

http://www.shippinggreatness.com

To comment or ask technical questions about this book, send email to:

bookquestions@oreilly.com

For more information about our books, courses, conferences, and news, see our website at *http://www.oreilly.com.*

Find us on Facebook: *http://facebook.com/oreilly*
Follow us on Twitter: *http://twitter.com/oreillymedia*
Watch us on YouTube: *http://www.youtube.com/oreillymedia*

Safari® Books Online

Safari Books Online (*www.safaribooksonline.com*) is an on-demand digital library that delivers expert content in both book and video form from the world's leading authors in technology and business.

Technology professionals, software developers, web designers, and business and creative professionals use Safari Books Online as their primary resource for research, problem solving, learning, and certification training.

Safari Books Online offers a range of product mixes and pricing programs for organizations, government agencies, and individuals. Subscribers have access to thousands of books, training videos, and prepublication manuscripts in one fully searchable database from publishers like O'Reilly Media, Prentice Hall Professional, Addison-Wesley Professional, Microsoft Press, Sams, Que, Peachpit Press, Focal Press, Cisco Press, John Wiley & Sons, Syngress, Morgan Kaufmann, IBM Redbooks, Packt, Adobe Press, FT Press, Apress, Manning, New Riders, McGraw-Hill, Jones & Bartlett, Course Technology, and dozens more. For more information about Safari Books Online, please visit us online.

Have it your way.

Get even more for your money.

Join the O'Reilly Community, and register the O'Reilly books you own. It's free, and you'll get:

- $4.99 ebook upgrade offer
- 40% upgrade offer on O'Reilly print books
- Membership discounts on books and events
- Free lifetime updates to ebooks and videos
- Multiple ebook formats, DRM FREE
- Participation in the O'Reilly community
- Newsletters
- Account management
- 100% Satisfaction Guarantee

Signing up is easy:

1. **Go to: oreilly.com/go/register**
2. **Create an O'Reilly login.**
3. **Provide your address.**
4. **Register your books.**

Note: English-language books only

To order books online:
oreilly.com/store

For questions about products or an order:
orders@oreilly.com

To sign up to get topic-specific email announcements and/or news about upcoming books, conferences, special offers, and new technologies:
elists@oreilly.com

For technical questions about book content:
booktech@oreilly.com

To submit new book proposals to our editors:
proposals@oreilly.com

O'Reilly books are available in multiple DRM-free ebook formats. For more information:
oreilly.com/ebooks

O'REILLY®

Spreading the knowledge of innovators   oreilly.com

CPSIA information can be obtained
at www.ICGtesting.com
Printed in the USA
BVOW08s1753161017
497788BV00028B/941/P